Lead From Who You Are

Lead From Who You Are

The Personal, People, and Process Rhythms of Meaningful Leadership

Dr. Joe Sanfelippo

ConnectEDD Publishing
Hanover, Pennsylvania

Copyright © 2026 by Joe Sanfelippo

All rights reserved. No part of this publication may be reproduced, distributed, or transmitted in any form or by any means, including photocopying, recording, or other electronic or mechanical methods, without the prior written permission of the publisher, except in the case of brief quotations embodied in critical reviews and certain other noncommercial uses permitted by copyright law. For permission requests, contact the publisher at: info@connecteddpublishing.com

This publication is available at discount pricing when purchased in quantity for educational purposes, promotions, or fundraisers. For inquiries and details, contact the publisher at: info@connecteddpublishing.com

Published by ConnectEDD Publishing LLC
Hanover, PA
www.connecteddpublishing.com

Cover Design: Kheila Casas

Lead From Who You Are —1st ed. Paperback
ISBN   979-8-9933700-3-3

Praise for *Lead From Who You Are*

This is not a book about becoming someone else. It's a book about understanding why WHO YOU ARE is everything in your leadership. In *Lead from Who You Are*, Joe Sanfelippo blends poignant storytelling with disciplined focus, showing readers how the consistent rhythm of their identity can elevate everything. This book transcends leadership. You'll feel it calling you to greatness, no matter your role. But the call is not distant or unattainable. It will resonate deeply, as your path forward becomes startlingly clear in every chapter. Addictively simple, yet profound. Genuine and grounded. Leadership is experienced in moments, and Joe Sanfelippo will help you decide who you want to be in all of yours.

–Dr. Brad Gustafson | MN Principal of the Year, author, and lover of life

Joe has a gift for taking the often-overwhelming idea of leadership and making it feel approachable—breaking it down into small, manageable practices grounded in strengths and self-awareness. One of the messages that has stayed with me most is his reminder that culture is built through the accumulation of a million small moments, and that being deliberate in how we lead is our best defense against the whirlwind of pressure, expectations, and daily demands that we face. Joe's work is both encouraging and motivating, inviting us to grow into the best version of ourselves while also extending grace along the way. It reassures us that we don't have to be someone else—or something bigger—to be enough.

–Dr. Carmen Maring | Principal

Dr. Joe Sanfelippo has been one of the most influential voices in my professional journey, and *Lead from Who You Are* continues to inspire me to strive to be my best self with a clear and consistent sense of who I am as a leader. In a profession that often creates self-doubt, anxiety, and inevitable imposter syndrome, where daily challenges can make you question if you are meant for the role, this book serves as a steady guide forward. Joe's Rhythm Leadership challenges you to reflect on who you are as a leader while offering tangible steps from a personal, people, and process approach to bring clarity to your work and purpose. He focuses on valuing people and honoring the meaningful moments that build trust through authentic relationships, while ensuring individuals feel supported and valued. The blend of Joe's personal experiences and powerful storytelling brings these leadership ideas to life in ways that are relatable and meaningful. Ultimately, *Lead from Who You Are* guides you in discovering your leadership core and leading with authenticity, offering a meaningful path for growth for leaders in any industry—starting from within.

–Tony Cattani | NASSP National High School Principal of the Year

Knowing who you are as a leader is tantamount to one's success, but it's often the easiest thing to lose when you're leading. In *Lead From Who You Are*, Dr. Joe Sanfelippo blends practical insights with timeless principles that help leaders see themselves in the stories and grow—sometimes with a smile, sometimes with a knowing head shake. It's the kind of book that stays with you, making you a better leader and strengthening the people you lead every day.

–Dr. Amber Teamann | Executive Director of Tech and Innovation, author, speaker

Lead From Who You Are is a timely reminder that the deepest work of leadership is inner work. Joe Sanfelippo gently but clearly invites leaders to root their influence in identity, not role, and to lead from rhythms that sustain rather than exhaust. Through the Personal, People, and Process rhythms, this book offers a wise, humane path for leading with presence, clarity, and care when the work feels heavy. This is not a call to become someone new, but an invitation to return to who you were always meant to be.

    –Damian LaCroix | WI Superintendent of the Year, Leadership Coach & Educational Consultant

There are leadership books that inform, and there are leadership books that reveal—and *Lead From Who You Are* by Joe Sanfelippo clearly falls into the latter category. This is not a book about leadership theory; it is a reflection of Joe's deep commitment to children, educators, leaders, and public education. Grounded in real stories from schools and classrooms, he captures both the joy and the weight of leadership at a time when educational leaders are facing unprecedented pressure. Rather than ignoring the complexity of today's work, the book offers something essential: permission to return to purpose and reconnect with who we are and why we chose this profession. Centered on the Personal, People, and Process rhythms, *Lead From Who You Are* reinforces that leadership is rooted not in position or authority, but in identity, presence, and everyday choices that shape culture. This book is not a call to do more—it is a call to lead with intention, authenticity, and humanity, serving as both a north star for new leaders and an anchor for those who feel stretched thin.

    –Eileen King | Executive Director, Maine School Superintendents Association

Joe captures a truth every leader eventually learns the hard way: you cannot lead others with clarity if you're unclear about yourself. *Lead From Who You Are* is thoughtful, practical, and deeply affirming—an essential read for anyone who wants to lead with integrity and presence.

    -Weston Kieshnick | Best-selling author, speaker, and coach

Whether you lead from a classroom, a boardroom, or anywhere in between, Joe reminds us that knowing who you are must come before anything you try to do. Joe's stories are honest, practical, and deeply human—the kind that people actually want to follow. This isn't just a leadership book; it's a blueprint for showing up with clarity, consistency, and heart.

> –Dr. Jessica Cabeen | Nationally Distinguished Principal, Author, Speaker, and Coach

Lead From Who You Are is a powerful reminder that meaningful leadership begins with understanding your values, purpose, and the identity you bring into every interaction. Through heartfelt stories and practical, human-centered rhythms, Dr. Sanfelippo beautifully reinforces that leadership isn't about titles or positions, but about presence, intention, and the everyday moments that build trust and shape culture. Through heartfelt stories and practical, human-centered rhythms, he illustrates how the smallest interactions can become the biggest movements in a school community. This book invites educators to reflect deeply, reconnect with their "WHO," and lead from a place of authenticity and clarity. It reminds us that when we are grounded in who we are, we show up differently—for ourselves, for our colleagues, and most importantly, for our students. *Lead From Who You Are* is essential reading for every educator because it affirms that leadership doesn't start with a role—it starts with YOU.

> –Dr. Tony Sinanis | NY Principal of the Year, Author, Speaker

Whether you are an experienced leader needing an essential grounding or a new leader in search of a tool to help you anchor your leadership in strong foundations, *Lead From Who You Are* will fortify you! Sanfelippo draws from a well of knowledge that applies research in leadership and personal development in his signature style of storytelling. It's as if reading with a friend as you focus on building the rhythms of leading yourself, others, and processes! A must read for all leaders.

> –Dr. Sarah Johnson | Author, Leadership Coach

Leadership doesn't begin with a role or a strategy; it begins with who you are. Sanfelippo reminds us that real influence comes not from position or charisma, but from consistency in how we show up when it matters most. This book pulls leadership out of theory and places it where it lives, in hallway conversations, quiet pauses, and the way people feel after an interaction. Joe doesn't offer a persona to perform; he offers a mirror, challenging leaders to align identity with behavior. If you're looking for a checklist, this isn't it. But if you're ready to lead with intention and understand why who you are lasts longer than what you say, this book will stay with you.

–Tom Murray | Director of Innovation, Future-Ready Schools, Best-Selling Author

Leadership requires a commitment to self-awareness, self-reflection, and the ability to make the appropriate leadership move in the right place at the right time. In *Lead From Who You Are*, Joe emphasizes the importance of knowing who you are as a leader, understanding who you serve, and recognizing the processes that must exist to create the leadership rhythm necessary for leading in complex, complicated systems. Joe challenges readers to get in sync with who they are as a leader so they can be what they need to be for the people and organizations they lead. With the ever-changing landscape that leaders face daily, it is important to establish connections built on consistency and decision-making grounded in trust and transparency. *Lead From Who You Are* is a reflective read that will help leaders build a solid foundation for impactful leadership.

–Sanée Bell, Ed.D. | Educational Leader, Author, Speaker

This book affirms what I have seen in schools and leaders across the country: leadership is personal before it is positional. Joe writes with heart and clarity about identity, belonging, and responsibility. *Lead*

From Who You Are pushes leaders to ask the right question—not "How am I leading?" but "Who am I leading as?" That shift changes everything.

> –Dr. J. Anderson | Executive Director, Missouri Association of Elementary/PK-8 School Principals

Dr. Joe Sanfelippo has written a masterclass in leadership that reminds us that what sets a leader apart isn't just what they know, but how they choose to do the work. If Lead from Where You Are gave people permission to lead, this prequel gives them the heart and habits to do it well. Joe is a phenomenal leader and an even better human—and this stellar book will stay with you long after you close the last page.

> –Jill Siler, Ed.D., TASA Deputy Executive Director, Author, Speaker

Dedication

To anyone along this leadership path who
has pushed me, pulled me, humbled me,
celebrated me, and still continues to help me lead…
You give this work purpose, and for that, I am full of gratitude.

Table of Contents

Foreword xvii

Preface: So Yeah…It's a Prequel xxi

PART I — The Personal Rhythm
Intention: Clarifying Purpose and Values

Chapter 1 *The Rhythms of Leadership* 3
When your leadership has a rhythm, your presence has purpose

Chapter 2 *The Mirror Test* 21
Seeing yourself clearly before leading others

Chapter 3 *Intentional Energy* 27
What you focus on grows; what you ignore fades

Chapter 4 *Finding Joy in the Work* 37
Joy isn't the reward; it's the strategy

Chapter 5 *Seeing Greatness around You* 45
What you recognize expands

Chapter 6 *Pace of Presence* 53
Leading in a way that matches the moment

Summary: *The Personal Rhythm* x

PART II — The People Rhythm
Connection: Building Trust and Collaboration

Chapter 7 Presence Over Position 67
Influence without authority

Chapter 8 Checking In With vs. Checking Up On 73
Leading through care, not compliance

Chapter 9 The Candy Hearts 81
The small signals that shape big perceptions

Chapter 10 Everyone's Favorite 85
Why consistency matters more than charisma

Chapter 11 Build Back Relationships 91
Repairing trust begins one intentional moment at a time

Chapter 12 Every Interaction Matters 97
The smallest moments create the longest memories

Chapter 13 In the Absence of Knowledge 103
You are either the narrator of your story or the character in someone else's

Chapter 14 The 30-Second Legacy 111
How brief moments leave lasting impressions

Summary: The People Rhythm 119

TABLE OF CONTENTS

PART III — The Process Rhythm
Direction: Moving People Forward

Chapter 15 *Model the Mission* 127
People follow what they see, not what they hear

Chapter 16 *The Expert's Space* 133
Great leaders don't walk into rooms to prove; they walk in to understand

Chapter 17 *Build Capacity, Not Dependence* 139
Grow leaders, not followers

Chapter 18 *Multiply the Good* 147
Extend the greatness you see

Chapter 19 *Moments Become Movements* 157
How brief moments turn into cultural shifts

Summary: *The Process Rhythm* 165

Conclusion 169
We're all in this thing together

Acknowledgements 173

About the Author 175

More from ConnectEDD Publishing 177

Foreword

Most days, my leadership begins in ordinary places. Sometimes at the front door of my school, sometimes in a hallway between classes, a brief conversation in the lunchroom, or a few minutes at an evening event. These moments are not part of any formal leadership plan, and I don't always get them right. But over time, I have learned that leadership happens when you *lean in*, when you truly notice, listen, and show up fully. People experience us in moments, not in titles.

As a principal, I have learned—often the hard way—that leadership is less about what I intend and more about how I show up.

A rushed interaction can undo trust.

A moment of presence can create it.

The smallest exchanges carry more weight than most leaders realize, and whether we are aware of it, every interaction becomes part of our leadership story.

Through the pages of this book, Joe reminds us that leadership begins with identity, understanding who we are before we attempt to lead others. In a profession that often rewards speed, output, and visibility, this book invites leaders to slow down and reflect. Not to do less, but to lead more intentionally. Not to add another initiative, but to anchor their work in clarity, connection, and purpose.

I've had the honor of knowing Joe for quite some time, but one moment has always stayed with me. When he came to speak to our district, he joined our administrative team for an informal barbecue at our superintendent's home the evening before his presentation. There was no agenda, no stage, and no expectation, just conversation, listening, and genuine connection. Long before he addressed a room full of educators, Joe was already doing the work he would later speak about. That consistency, between belief and behavior, is what gives this book its power.

What Joe describes here does not stop at the school doors. I have felt the truth of these rhythms in my personal life as well, especially as a mother. The same presence that builds trust in a hallway matters around the dinner table. The same energy we carry into meetings shows up at home at the end of long days. The same attention to joy, intentional energy, and noticing others translates across both work and family life. Leadership identity is not something we turn on at work and set down at home; it is who we are, everywhere we show up. By choosing to *lean in*, to be fully present, attentive, and engaged in the small moments, we shape relationships, culture, and a sense of belonging in ways we often don't fully see.

Through the Personal, People, and Process rhythms, Joe offers leaders a way to steady themselves amid complexity. *Personal Rhythm* centers us in self-awareness, intentional energy, and joy. *People Rhythm* reminds us that leadership is fundamentally relational and built through trust, recognition, and meaningful connection. *Process Rhythm* sustains momentum by keeping work manageable, meaningful, and magnetic, connecting what has been done to what comes next. Together, these rhythms move leadership from something we *do* to something we *live*.

What I appreciate most about this work is that it honors the small moments. The check-in before a problem escalates. The follow-up after a difficult conversation. The decision to notice and name greatness in others. These are the moments that shape culture, often long before any formal plan does. Joe challenges us to recognize that influence is inevitable, and to choose whether we will use it intentionally or accidentally.

FOREWORD

This book is not a prescription. It is an invitation. An invitation to pause before entering a room and consider the energy you bring with you. To look honestly in the mirror and reflect on how your values show up under pressure. To choose presence over position, connection over convenience, and joy as a daily practice rather than a distant reward.

Leadership does not live in grand gestures. It lives in the everyday choices we make about who we are and how we show up. As you move through your own days, at school, at home, and in your community, pause to notice moments that matter. Small acts of presence, connection, and joy may seem ordinary in the moment, but they are where leadership truly lives. *Lean in* to these moments, lead with intention, and allow the rhythms of your own life to guide you. When you do, the moments you create will ripple farther than you ever imagined, and others will carry the memory of your leadership long after you have left the room.

Dr. Beth Houf
Proud Principal, Capital City High School
2022 NASSP National Principal of the Year

PREFACE

Who You are Matters More than Where You Are

It was early in the morning before the buzz of kids and teachers ran through the building. I liked walking the hallways before the start of the school day and making quick connections with staff members, kids who were there for weight training, or those who had been dropped off early. One of the classrooms I walked into often was Dave's. We'd talk about school, growing up in the '80s and early '90s, the Green Bay Packers, or college basketball, and I always had to pull myself away because I knew he had things to do that didn't include deep discussions with the superintendent, though he always made me feel welcome.

Dave is the kind of teacher every school leader wishes they had more of. He loves the kids, the work, and the community. People trust him. Staff go to him for advice. They follow his lead without him ever asking them to. So almost without thinking, I said, "Hey Dave, you should go into administration. You'd be great at it." He shrugged it off with a quick, "No, not really for me" and we moved on. It was a ten-second moment in a ten-minute conversation.

The next day, I walked by his room again and stopped in to say hi. As he sat at his desk and we talked informally for a few minutes, he paused and said, "What you said yesterday really bothered me."

I was caught off guard. "Tell me more about that?"

He took a breath and said, "This is what I want to do. I want to be the best teacher I can be. When you asked me about administration, it felt like you thought I should want something else."

I saw someone with natural influence and assumed that meant he wanted something different. In hindsight, I can see that assumption said more about me than it did about him. He wasn't chasing a title or the next thing. He was chasing excellence in the role he loved. He wasn't trying to be a different version of himself. He was trying to be the best version of himself. Simply starting the conversation by knowing and valuing who he was would have helped me understand where he wanted to go. Here's the part that stayed with me far longer than the conversation itself: I hadn't taken the time to understand myself well enough to see what was actually happening. I wasn't leading from who I was, I was leading from a version of leadership I thought I was supposed to embody. Because I wasn't grounded in my own *who*, I projected my assumptions onto him instead of noticing who he was trying to become.

A few years ago, I wrote a book titled *Lead From Where You Are*, and my hope was that it gave people permission to lead from wherever they were. The tools focused more on how to lead from any position and less on the person in that position. What I missed, and what Dave showed me, is that permission means very little if you don't understand the person you're giving the permission to. *That's when it hit me: you can't lead people if you don't understand who they are, and you can't lead from where you are if you don't first understand who you are.* This book, *Lead From Who You Are*, is the origin story I didn't realize we needed. It's the identity work required before any leadership strategy has a chance of sticking.

The Who Behind the Action

As I kept talking with leaders across the country, a similar pattern began to emerge—not in their roles, but in their reflections. People didn't want leaders who had all the answers. They wanted leaders who understood them, who were human enough to listen, learn, and adjust. The truth is, you can't understand others if you've skipped the work of understanding yourself. It is almost impossible to see the work through someone else's lens if your own is blurry, borrowed, or built from someone else's expectations.

Leadership at its core begins with knowing *who* you are before you ever show up for anyone else. It's carrying a core set of values that doesn't just guide your decisions; it steadies your presence. It's walking into rooms with clarity instead of performance. It's leading in a way that lets people breathe because your consistency removes the guesswork. *When leaders show up anchored, steady, and true to themselves, a rhythm begins to form, a predictable cadence people can trust.*

What People are Really Asking For

As I traveled, I kept hearing the same kinds of stories, no matter the size of the district, the community, or the job title. A paraprofessional in California who was literally changing the lives of students by finding food for their families outside of school, yet got into her car every day and cried as she left school because she didn't feel like she was doing enough. A veteran teacher in Tennessee who was brilliant in the classroom but hesitated to speak up in meetings because she wasn't sure her voice carried any weight. A first-year principal in Texas who was reluctant to talk about the great things happening in his school because he didn't want to ostracize himself from other principals in the district. A superintendent in Florida who was under so much pressure from her board that she lost sight of the leader she had always been and wanted to be. Different roles, same uncertainty. Not about their values, those were clear. The uncertainty was about how to translate who they were into actions that mattered for the people around them. And I didn't just hear these stories; I saw pieces of them in my own leadership. Their struggles reveal the same truth: you can't lead confidently on the outside if you're unsure of who you are on the inside.

People weren't tired of leaders; they were tired of leaders who didn't understand the people they were leading. They were tired of leaders who made decisions without knowing the stories of the faces in front of them, leaders who led from a distance instead of from their own humanity. They weren't bad leaders; they were ungrounded ones. Ungrounded because they may have known who they wanted to be, but hadn't yet figured out how to live that identity in real time with the people they served.

This book exists to help you bridge *who* you are with the opportunities, demands, and challenges of the people around you. People need leaders with a clear, consistent sense of who they want to be and the ability to take that aspirational best self and use it to see and serve others. But that only happens when you first understand your own *who*. I've tried skipping that step, and all it does is pull you into chasing approval, trying to make everyone happy, and losing yourself in the process. Start with your own *who* so you can bring your best self to every person and every situation, as a listener, as a supporter, and as a leader worth following.

The internal work matters. Not the soft, theoretical kind, but the practical, foundational kind. Knowing your core values, leading the person in the mirror so you're strong enough to lead a room. Seeing the greatness in yourself, others, and the organization you may lead. Finding joy when the work gets heavy and building habits that keep you steady. This is the work that makes leadership human and real, and it starts with *who* you are.

A Prequel that Propels You Forward

So yes, this is the prequel, but it's the one that makes sense. This is the book that reveals the core behind the action, the identity behind the influence, and the *who* behind every *where* you'll ever lead. Because when you know who you are, you lead better where you are, and the people around you feel the difference immediately. Thanks, Dave. Let's go to work.

PART I

The Personal Rhythm

*Intention:
Clarifying Purpose and Values*

CHAPTER 1

The Rhythms of Leadership

**When your leadership has a rhythm,
your presence has a purpose**

*"Blessed are the flexible,
for they shall not be bent out of shape."*
—Robert Schuller

If you've ever picked up a guitar for the first time, you know two things immediately:

(1) it's definitely not going to sound like a guitar commercial, and
(2) no matter how hard you strum, it will never sound like a piano.

Depending on how many hours you've spent with a guitar, the sound that comes out will be either beautifully familiar…or the kind of noise that makes everyone in the room look for the nearest exit. The more you play it, the more predictable it becomes. You start to know its rhythms. You can feel what's coming before the sound even hits the air.

And the people listening, even if they don't know music, can tell when you've found your groove and when you're just hoping the next chord won't betray you.

Leadership works the same way. When your rhythm becomes an instrument of consistency, people trust that you are who you say you are, even when they don't necessarily love where you're trying to take them. They can feel the steadiness. They can hear the predictability. They know the rhythm.

That's why you don't pick up a new role and suddenly become a different instrument. You get better by understanding the one you already have, by learning how it plays, how it resonates, and how it sounds to the people around you.

Leadership isn't about becoming someone new; it's about uncovering who you already are and choosing to lead from that place. The most effective leaders I know rely on presence, clarity, and purpose. They understand that leading begins with the self, knowing what drives you, what grounds you, and what gives you energy when the excitement of something new fades.

That's the heart of this book. *Lead From Who You Are* is about finding the rhythm that keeps you steady, the mindset that keeps you grounded, and the courage that keeps you growing. It's about leading with authenticity, because when you lead from who you are, people don't just follow your words; they trust your actions.

Jimmy Casas, a finalist for national secondary principal of the year and a Washington Post best-selling author of the book *Culturize*, talks about going back to the Interview Chair when you lose your way. He thinks the person in the interview is the best version of us, so when we struggle, we need to return to that version. I agree with this way of thinking. No one sits in an interview and says they are going to walk past things in the hallway that hurt the organization's culture. People don't tell a hiring committee they will show up in the morning carrying the resentment from a meeting the day before. Not many people tell an interview committee they are not going to support those they lead, but sometimes we lose our way and need to be brought back. The person in the interview chair is who you want to be. It is why you wanted to be in that room. It is the core of who you are. Start there and make sure *who* you aspire to be is someone worth following, just like you did in that chair.

Leadership rarely unfolds in neat, predictable lines. It moves in seasons, cycles, and patterns. In moments of clarity followed by moments of chaos, stretches of momentum followed by stretches where everything feels harder than it should. Early in my career, I kept trying to "get it right," to find the perfect strategy or the perfect routine that would hold steady no matter what the day threw at me. But leadership doesn't work like that. People don't work like that. Schools definitely don't work like that.

What I learned, slowly and usually the hard way, is that leadership behaves more like rhythm than routine. Routines break the moment the unexpected shows up. Rhythms bend with it. Routines depend on everything going as planned. Rhythms help you stay steady when nothing goes as planned. Rhythms don't demand perfection; they help you find your footing again when you've lost it.

That's why I stopped trying to build a perfect system and started looking for patterns that showed up in my best days, the days when I felt grounded, the interactions that moved people forward, the moments when I could feel myself leading from who I was, not who I thought I was supposed to be. I realized that my best leadership wasn't random. It had a beat to it. A flow. A rhythm I returned to without even knowing I was doing it.

And when I paid attention to that rhythm, it made everything else clearer. It helped me understand why some days felt aligned, and others felt scattered. It helped me see where I drifted and where I needed to come back. And it helped me create consistency not just for myself but for the people who needed me to be steady, even when the world around us wasn't.

Rhythms aren't rigid. They're fluid and allow you to slow down without stopping, adjust without overcorrecting, and lead with intention even when the day tries to pull you into reaction. They don't ask you to be perfect; they ask you to be present, and presence is where the real work happens. Presence isn't just showing up; it's showing up with purpose in a way that includes a consistent connection to who you want to be.

That's why this book centers on three core rhythms: Personal, People, and Process. They emerged not from theory but from the lived experience of twenty-six years in a school building, from mistakes and course corrections, from conversations in hallways and reflections in late-night parking lots. They aren't strategies you memorize. They're patterns you return to. They're the beats that hold your leadership steady when everything else starts to accelerate.

When you start to recognize your rhythm, you begin to recognize yourself again. I think of them as the **Personal Rhythm, the People Rhythm, and the Process Rhythm**—three ways of seeing the work that help you lead from who you are, not just what your role requires.

The Personal Rhythm: Intention, Connection, Direction

The personal rhythm is the heartbeat of leadership. It starts with intention, being clear about who you are and how you want to show up long before you walk into the room. When your intention is grounded, you move differently. You listen differently. You respond differently. You don't lead from impulse; you lead from your personal identity.

That intention becomes connection. People may respond to titles for a while, but there is a very low ceiling to that way of thinking. The organizations that move mountains have leaders who understand that those they lead respond to presence. Connection is how people *feel* around you, and more importantly, how people feel about themselves when they're around you. When your identity is steadier than your environment, you build quiet trust—in small moments, not big speeches.

And those two pieces, intention and connection, give you direction not just for the organization, but for yourself. You stop running from fire to fire and instead start walking with purpose. Direction is clarity in motion, the ability to move people forward because you've first grounded yourself.

That's the rhythm behind the most meaningful leaders I've ever met. You see it in the ones who know how to steady themselves even in situations that are not steady. You see it in the ones who are anchored in purpose and identity, which give courage to everyone around them. You see it in the ones who don't let urgency shape their identity, who don't let other people's emotions dictate their responses. You see it in the ones who understand that leadership isn't something you switch on and off; it's who you are, wherever you go.

Personal-driven leadership shows up quietly. It shows up in the way you pause before reacting. In the way you walk into a hard conversation with curiosity instead of defensiveness. In the way you anchor yourself before you step into a room, so you don't absorb the chaos you're walking into. *Leaders who return to their Personal rhythm don't avoid hard things; they simply refuse to let those moments rewire who they are.*

That rhythm doesn't make you perfect. It makes you predictable in the best possible way. People don't need leaders who have all the answers; they need leaders they can count on. They need to know how you'll show up even when you're tired, pressured, frustrated, or stretched thin. When your identity guides you rather than emotion, people feel safer bringing you the truth. They feel safer taking risks, and more importantly, safer being themselves. Grounded identity creates grounded rooms. That rhythm shows up through three intentional choices—Intention, Connection, and Direction. Each one building on the last and shaping how people experience your leadership.

Intention is the starting point. It's the quiet decision you make long before anyone sees your work. Intention asks the question every great leader returns to: How do I want people to experience me? Not as a title or a role, but as a human being who shows up with purpose. When you lead with intention, your choices have weight. Your presence has meaning. And your actions begin aligning with the story you want others to tell when you're not in the room. Intention doesn't require perfection—it requires awareness. It's knowing why you do what you do and choosing to lead with clarity rather than by accident.

Connection is where intention comes to life. If intention shapes how you show up, connection shapes how people feel when you do. Leadership lives or dies in relationships, not the surface-level ones built on position, but the deep, steady ones built on trust. Connection is crafted through small conversations, consistent presence, and the willingness to see people before you lead them. When leaders connect first, everything else becomes easier: feedback goes deeper, collaboration is more meaningful, and people feel safe enough to bring their best selves to the work. Connection is about being human enough to care.

Direction is what turns purpose and people into progress. It's easy to stay stuck in inspiration. It's harder to move a group of people toward something that actually matters. Direction isn't only about pointing the way; it's about walking it with people. It's about clarity that reduces confusion. It's about alignment that removes friction. It's about forward momentum built not on pressure, but on shared understanding. Direction reminds us that leadership isn't just about making people feel good; it's about helping them grow, helping them move, and helping them reach a place they couldn't have reached alone.

Intention grounds you.
Connection strengthens you.
Direction moves you.

Together, they form a rhythm that anchors your leadership in your personal identity, not in position, not in pressure, not in performance, but in who you are at your core. It's a rhythm you return to on the days that feel steady and the days that feel like chaos. A rhythm that helps you show up with clarity, humanity, and purpose, one interaction, conversation, and decision at a time.

The PEOPLE RHYTHM: Recognize, Acknowledge, Extend Framework

If the personal rhythm centers who you are, the people rhythm centers who you lead. It's the reminder that leadership is not a solo act; it's a relational experience. No matter how skilled, organized, or visionary a leader may be, nothing moves without people. The commitment and distance people move are directly related to the connection they have to the person asking them to move, which is always better and farther when they feel connected enough to trust that person.

The people rhythm begins with presence. Not just showing up, but *how* you show up. You can have the clearest intention in the world, but if people don't feel seen, valued, and understood in your presence, they won't join you in the work. Presence is the quiet signal that tells people whether they're safe, supported, and respected. It's not dramatic or loud. It's often built in the unscheduled moments, in a hallway, after a meeting, during a transition, or in the five seconds it takes to pause and make eye contact. Those seemingly small moments are where connection either strengthens or fractures.

When leaders understand the people rhythm, they stop thinking of trust as something they earn once and keep forever. Trust becomes something they continuously invest in. It becomes less about managing tasks and more about tending to relationships. People want leaders who listen before they judge, who seek to understand before they offer direction, and who walk into spaces believing in the expertise of the people already there. When leaders operate from that posture, the environment changes. Anxiety lowers, and collaboration increases. Conversations are honest, and people become more willing to take risks, speak honestly, and contribute fully.

Connection is rarely built in the big moments. It's built in the dozens of smaller ones that happen when no one is "performing." Those are the moments when people quietly decide if their leader is someone they can trust. If what you say matches what you model. If your presence brings steadiness instead of pressure. If your questions feel like curiosity instead of criticism. Every one of those moments adds up.

When I was growing up, the ability to work well with people was considered a "soft skill." An add-on to other pieces of leadership that were somehow more important. The word "soft" evokes a litany of negative perceptions when it comes to leadership. The people rhythm isn't soft work; it's essential work. It's the daily practice of reminding people through your actions, tone, and consistency that they matter. When people feel supported and valued, they give more of themselves, not because they have to, but because they want to. And when that happens, your entire organization breathes easier. Communication flows more naturally. Feedback feels safer. Problem-solving becomes more collaborative. The culture becomes lighter, more connected, and more human. That environment makes the good days great, but also makes the bad days better.

This rhythm is the bridge between who you are and what you hope to accomplish with others. It's what transforms leadership from something you *do* into something people *experience*. And that's where the next rhythm comes in—the practical, human framework that gives structure to how leaders bring this people-centered approach to life.

Recognize is the entry point to the people's rhythm. It's the quiet commitment to pay attention, to look for what's right, what's improving, and what's worth celebrating. Recognition isn't about catching someone doing something "perfect." It's about noticing the effort, the courage, the small step forward. When leaders practice recognition consistently, they communicate, "I see you, even when you think no one does."

Acknowledge takes recognition a step further by naming what you see. When a leader says, "I noticed how you handled that conversation," or "I watched how you stayed composed when it mattered," they turn an invisible moment into a meaningful one. Acknowledgment validates not just the action, but the person. It builds belief. It helps people understand why their work matters. And when acknowledgment is specific, it becomes a form of fuel—quiet, steady, personal.

Extend is what turns individual moments into collective culture. It's when leaders carry stories of greatness to people who didn't witness them. When you tell someone, "Let me tell you what I saw today," you create ripples of positivity that travel farther than the moment itself. Extension shows people that their work isn't just appreciated, it's worth sharing. It builds pride. It builds unity. It builds momentum. And when leaders extend consistently, it becomes part of the organizational identity: we share stories of greatness here.

> Recognize creates awareness.
> Acknowledge creates belonging.
> Extend creates culture.

Together, they form a rhythm that strengthens relationships, deepens trust, and transforms everyday interactions into the foundation of a thriving, human-centered workplace. It is the everyday, steady practice that allows leaders to lead not just with skill, but with humanity—rooted in who they are and grounded in the people who make the work possible.

The PROCESS RHYTHM: Manageable, Meaningful, Magnetic Framework

If the personal rhythm centers who you are and the people rhythm centers who you lead, the process rhythm centers how you keep going. Leadership isn't about being great once; it's a sustained movement. And sustaining anything over time requires more than motivation or passion. It requires structure, clarity, and a rhythm you can return to when energy, excitement, or momentum fade. Most leaders start strong. There is often excitement about change or hope that things are going to go in a different direction. Think about press conferences for coaching positions. There are a ton of leaders who win the press conference. Create excitement for what is to come. It energizes the fan base and gets the message boards buzzing. That isn't the hard part. The hard part is staying strong long enough to make the work meaningful.

Processes don't exist to constrain leaders. They exist to carry leaders. They reduce the emotional burden of decision fatigue. They create predictability in moments that feel chaotic. They keep you anchored to purpose when the natural rhythms of the year push you toward drift. And most importantly, good processes give people a better chance to succeed, not because the work gets easier, but because the path forward becomes clearer.

The process rhythm shows up in the small, repeatable actions that give structure to your leadership. It's how you start your day, how you reset when something throws you off, how you circle back to people, how you create momentum, and how you return to the habits that reconnect you to purpose. When leaders build processes that match who they are—not who they think they're supposed to be—they create a leadership experience that is sustainable instead of exhausting, grounded instead of reactive, and human instead of hurried. When they chase a persona they never were and ask a group to do the same, it always–and I mean always–catches up with them.

That's where the Manageable, Meaningful, and Magnetic framework comes in. These three mindsets don't replace process, they shape it. They keep the work from becoming overwhelming, disconnected, or stale. They help leaders create systems that are strong enough to support people and flexible enough to honor humanity.

Manageable is the first anchor. It reminds leaders that people won't start something they already believe is too big. Manageable doesn't mean easy. It doesn't mean lowering expectations. It means designing the next step small enough that people can take it on their hardest days, not just their best ones. When a process feels manageable, people are more willing to begin.

Meaningful is the momentum keeper. It connects the process to something deeper. Leaders can create dozens of systems, but if none of them connect to purpose, the energy fades quickly. When people understand why the work matters, when they feel it is tied to identity, impact, or personal value, they stay with it longer. Meaningful work inspires more effort because of the personal connection it has to those involved.

Magnetic is what makes the work come alive and what keeps it from drifting into isolated initiatives that confuse or exhaust the people you serve. Magnetic systems connect what has been done to what comes next. They build continuity instead of chaos. They create alignment instead of fragmentation. In organizations struggling with "flavor of the month" leadership, where each new book (not including this one, of course), workshop, or initiative becomes the next big thing, Magnetic becomes the antidote. It ensures that every new step reinforces the last one, that the work builds instead of stacks, and that people can actually see how today's effort leads to tomorrow's growth.

Magnetic isn't just good for the people being led, it becomes a litmus test for the leader. If a new idea doesn't connect to the story you're already telling, the system you're already building, or the purpose your people already believe in, it's not magnetic. And if it's not magnetic, it won't last. When leaders embrace Magnetic as a filter, they stop adding initiatives out of urgency and start building processes out of coherence. They create momentum out of purpose.

When leaders embrace processes that are manageable, meaningful, and magnetic, they stop relying on motivation alone. Instead, they build structures that carry them through the predictable highs and lows. They make the work startable, sustainable, and energizing for themselves and for the people they lead. They create a leadership rhythm that doesn't just survive the difficult days, but stays steady because of them.

The process rhythm is not about rigid routines or perfectly planned systems. It's about anchoring your leadership in habits that give you—and everyone around you—a better chance to succeed consistently. It's the rhythm that keeps you grounded, keeps you moving, and keeps you connected to who you want to be, long after the initial excitement fades.

Bringing the Rhythms Together

Leadership doesn't live in a title, a strategy, or a perfectly crafted plan; it lives in rhythm. Not the rhythm of schedules or initiatives, but the rhythm of how you show up, how you connect, and how you sustain movement over time. When you understand the three rhythms—personal, people, and process, *you stop treating leadership like a list of things to accomplish and start experiencing it as a way of being.*

The personal rhythm is where it begins. It steadies you. It centers you. It reminds you that leadership is personal long before it is positional. When you lead with intention, people experience consistency instead of confusion. When you stay rooted in who you are, the work doesn't shake you as easily. Grounding yourself in personal identity isn't self-focus, it's self-alignment. It's choosing to show up on purpose instead of by accident.

The people rhythm takes that internal clarity and turns it outward. Leadership is, at its core, relational. People don't follow energy they can't feel or trust. Connection happens in the conversation before the meeting, the tone of the email, and the way you listen when you're already tired. When leaders connect first, they lead differently. They communicate with more empathy, give feedback with more trust, and create environments where people can bring their full selves to the work, not just the part that fits the job description. The people rhythm makes leadership less about managing tasks and more about lifting people.

The process rhythm is what keeps the work alive. *Personal identity keeps you grounded, connection keeps you trusted, but process keeps you moving.* Manageable steps make growth possible. Meaningful work fuels persistence. And magnetic systems prevent the drift that happens when leaders chase the newest idea instead of building on what already exists. When leaders move through the process rhythm with intention, they create momentum that lasts, momentum that doesn't collapse the moment something becomes difficult.

Each rhythm matters on its own, but the real power comes when they work together. When your identity is clear, people feel safe around you. When people feel safe, they connect more deeply. When they connect more deeply, they move with more clarity and purpose. That's the rhythm of leadership: steady, human, repeatable.

To succeed, you need something more than motivation. You need a structure that helps you stay consistent when the noise of leadership gets loud. That structure comes from reflecting on what you have done and building frameworks–simple, repeatable systems that allow you to think, decide, and act with intention. Reflection will occur after each of the following chapters with a **Core Value Connection**. This will give you a chance to review the chapter and see what actions will give you the most momentum, always going back to **who** you are as a leader. This book uses Manageable, Meaningful and Magnetic activities that speak to the specific chapter, and just as importantly, the rhythm to which it is attached. This entire manuscript is an attempt to model what you can do in your space and in doing so I want to make sure you have a sequence that contributes to the frameworks and systems you build that reflect your core values.

Why Frameworks Matter

When we lose our way, we need a structure to help bring us back. Just as my car reminds me when I am veering a bit too far from my lane, frameworks afford me the opportunity to stay true to who I am. I don't think of frameworks as rules as much as I think of them as reminders. They slow you down long enough to ensure your actions reflect your values and that your decisions align with your direction. They serve as mental guardrails that help you lead with focus rather than in reaction to events as they occur

A solid framework is clear enough to remember and flexible enough to apply anywhere. It keeps you from chasing the next new thing and helps you invest your energy in what matters most. When done well, frameworks don't limit you, they actually free you. They free your time, but they also free your mindset by providing continuity. They give you a consistent language for how you lead and help others see what consistency looks like in you.

Throughout this book, you will see direct references to the three frameworks listed above because I believe they can serve as an anchor for the work of leadership, but please understand that I don't have a monopoly on what framework should be used in your organization. They are simply meant to spark reflection and action and help you build your own rhythm of leadership rooted in who you are and what your people need.

Building Your Own Frameworks

Frameworks are one of the anchors of leadership. They give structure to what often feels like chaos. At their core, frameworks are repeatable ways of thinking that guide our actions when emotions, uncertainty, or exhaustion start to take over. They don't tell us *what* to do as much as they remind us *how* we want to do it. How to show up, how to communicate, and how to stay grounded when everything else feels like it's moving too fast.

A good framework slows you down so your leadership can speed up. It creates consistency, especially when you're leading teams that rely on clarity and alignment. The goal isn't to add more structure for the sake of control. It's to build a rhythm that keeps you steady and helps others feel confident in where you're headed.

I worked with a leader who was and is a fantastic person. She was resilient, energetic, and cared deeply about the organization. The problem was sometimes that energy and care turned into feeling the need to respond to issues immediately and therefore coming off as rigid and lacking empathy for those involved. She was trying to get people the answers to their questions immediately so as to not overwhelm them with the weight and wait of the conversation, but instead, a passionate reaction in the moment, good or bad, impacted the reaction from the other person involved. When we talked about taking a breath, asking for clarifying questions, and always saying she would get the information she needed and follow up as soon as she had an answer, it slowed the process to a place where a better decision was made, in a less rigid way, with a tone that could move people forward. Simple changes that slow us down, but are intentional actions that give us the best chance of leading effectively

Creating your own framework starts with reflection, not instruction. Here's how to begin:

1. **Name What Matters Most**
   Think about the moments when you've led at your best. What guided your decisions? What patterns show up in how you treat people or solve problems? Those themes often become the foundation of a framework.

2. **Distill It Into Three**
   Three is the magic number, easy to remember, hard to ignore. When you can name your principles in threes (*like Intention, Connection, Direction, or Recognize, Acknowledge, Extend, or Manageable, Meaningful, Magnetic*), you create language that others can repeat and rally around.

3. **Define the Behavior**
   Frameworks aren't slogans, they're systems for action. Once you name the parts, define what each one *looks like in motion*. If your framework includes "Connect," describe how you do it: morning check-ins, handwritten notes, walking the halls with purpose.

4. **Share and Revisit**
   Frameworks grow with you. When you share them with your team, you create shared language and expectations. When you revisit them regularly, you give yourself permission to evolve.

Frameworks aren't just tools for leadership; they're tools for life. They help us show up the same way on hard days as we do on easy ones. The best ones don't make you someone new; they help you see more of who you already are.

Framework Reflection Guide

Frameworks help you organize what matters most, so you can act with clarity rather than react out of habit. The goal isn't to build something that sounds perfect, it's to create something that helps you *show up on purpose*. Use the prompts below to start shaping a framework that reflects your leadership and your life.

1. Recognize Your Core Patterns
Think back on the last few months. When were you at your best as a leader, colleague, or friend? What were you doing, and more importantly, *how* were you doing it?

Reflection Prompt: What three words describe the way you want people to feel after they interact with you?

2. Name the Anchors
Look for themes in what you wrote. Maybe you lead through listening, encouragement, and follow-through. Maybe your strength is building trust, setting direction, and celebrating progress. Group your patterns and start naming your anchors; these will become the parts of your framework.

Reflection Prompt: If someone shadowed you for a week, what consistent actions or attitudes would they notice?

3. Define the Action
Turn each anchor into something you can *see*. How will you live it out tomorrow, next week, or in the next conversation you have? Keep it simple and repeatable.

Reflection Prompt: For each part of your framework, what's one behavior that shows you're living it?

When you finish, you'll have a personal framework, a simple, repeatable structure that helps you lead with intention. Don't worry about making it perfect; make it *real to you*, because **who** you want to be can be the rhythm your people rally around. A purpose and identity that's so real, relatable, and aspirational that it elevates the intention of others. The most powerful frameworks aren't the ones that impress people, they're the ones that keep you grounded when life gets loud.

CHAPTER 2

The Mirror Test

Seeing yourself clearly before leading others

*"Until you make the unconscious conscious,
it will direct your life, and you will call it fate."*
— Carl Jung

For those people who have never lived in Wisconsin during the winter months, let me break it down for you. You walk outside in December or January and it's minus whatever, the kind of cold where the actual number doesn't matter because your body has already stopped negotiating with you. The second you step out, your eyes start to tear up, and the longer you stay out there, those tears freeze right to your eyelashes. You start walking faster just to get to the building, but the sidewalks are icy or the snow hasn't been shoveled, so now you're trudging through frozen snow piles like you're competing in a winter obstacle course. By the time you get inside, you're not showing up like a leader, you're showing up like someone who just survived.

One morning, someone hit me with a cheerful "Good morning!" right inside that door. What came out of my mouth technically counted as a greeting but definitely did not sound like the leader I intended to be. Nothing had happened. No crisis. No emergency. No dramatic moment. I was just cold, tired, and reacting to something I had zero control over. But that tiny reaction ended up shaping the way that person experienced me, and probably shaped the tone of their morning, too. Some leadership moments don't show up with a title, a meeting agenda, or a big decision. They show up long before anyone realizes a "leadership moment" is even happening. Most leaders I talk to don't get tripped up by the big moments. The big moments come with meetings, prep, agendas, and warning signs. It's the small, unscripted stuff, the thirty seconds between the parking lot and the front door, that ends up shaping how people remember you. Those moments need awareness. And that's where the "Mirror Test" begins.

In the previous chapter, we talked about creating frameworks and how naming what matters, defining the behavior, and revisiting it consistently helps you return to who you are. The Mirror Test is one of those frameworks. It's simple and direct in the way the best frameworks usually are. It asks four questions that tell you the truth about the version of you walking into the room:

1. Who am I right now?
2. Does this reaction reflect my values?
3. Am I responding from my personal identity or from the stress of the moment?
4. Will people experience consistency or confusion when they walk toward me?

If all you do is slow down long enough to consider these questions, your leadership immediately becomes more grounded. You're not aiming for perfection; you're aiming for awareness of who you want to be. I hear versions of this from leaders everywhere. They'll say some version of, "I didn't love that my reaction to something I couldn't control became the thing people remembered." And they're right. People rarely remember the cause. They remember the reaction. The tone, the sigh, the look, the energy that wasn't meant for them but landed on them anyway. Whether you're leading a department of two, a classroom, an office team, or a school, or a district, people follow the version of you that shows up most consistently,

> **people follow the version of you that shows up most consistently**

not the version that only appears on your best days. The Mirror Test is how you close that gap between who you are once and who you are with every interaction.

I learned how much this mattered a few years ago when I got a knock on my front door at nine o'clock on a Friday night. A man I'd never seen before asked, "Are you Joe Sanfelippo?" Then he handed me a packet of papers and walked away like it was no big deal. The first page said, "The People v. Joe Sanfelippo, Superintendent of the Fall Creek School District." My name. Page one. He had five more stops that night to deliver papers to our school board members. I heard from a few people that there was a chance of a lawsuit, but all the preparation in the world doesn't get you ready for the day someone shows up with the paperwork. We weren't being sued for anything unusual. It was a practice nearly every nearby district was using during the pandemic where schools were coming back into session. But for whatever reason, we were the target. And it weighed on me. It followed me everywhere, into conversations, into meetings, even into my sleep.

People would ask, "Hey Joe, how are you doing?" and in my head I'd think, *"I'm being sued in federal court, Sharon, how do you think I'm doing?"* I didn't want anyone to feel awkward asking questions, but I couldn't really tell them anything because of the legal implications, and I didn't want to pretend I was OK, so I started avoiding people. I kept my head down. I stayed quiet. Whether I meant to or not, I walked through school as the stressed-out version of myself instead of the leader I wanted to be. None of that matched my values. I'm not a shy person; in fact, sometimes I can be too much for people. I try to bring a lot of energy to every interaction, whether I'm walking down the hallway, celebrating staff and students, or telling a dad joke a little too loud in a public place to get the reaction of my kids. That's who I am. That's the version of me people expect. But I let it push me into the exact opposite persona. People around me noticed right away because I didn't go from low energy to no energy; I went from high energy to no energy, and on the days when I tried to dial the energy back up, it probably looked like I was overcompensating. Either way, it wasn't me, and it wasn't the identity I wanted to live out loud. I wasn't responding from who I was. I was responding from the pressure I was carrying. Pressure always tries to pull leaders off tempo, and if you're not careful, the noise around you becomes louder than the rhythm within you. Returning to your rhythm is what brings you back into alignment. It took an eight-year-old on a school playground to be the mirror for me.

One afternoon, while I was walking across the playground with my head down, stuck in my own thoughts, one of our elementary kids yelled, "SANFELIPPO! LOOK UP! WATCH ME!" Then he took off running. Full speed, arms pumping, giant smile, laughing…it was so pure. So I looked up. I watched him run. I cheered. And in that simple moment, everything that had been weighing on me loosened just enough for me to feel like myself again. It didn't fix the lawsuit. It didn't remove the pressure. But it reminded me who I was. It reminded me what mattered. It reminded me that I needed to show up as the version of myself my people needed.

That's the power of the Mirror Test. It's not dramatic or complicated. It's the pause that lets you check whether your identity and your presence match. No leadership book or strategy can do that work for you. It begins the moment you check in with yourself.

When your identity is clear, your leadership becomes more consistent. When it's consistent, people trust you. And when people trust you, everything else, teams, culture, direction, and momentum becomes easier to move.

> Being aware doesn't instantly change the world, but it does change your place in it.

Being aware doesn't instantly change the world, but it does change your place in it. You stop walking into a room trying to control everything and start paying attention to what the room actually needs from you. It steadies you. It keeps your leadership grounded instead of reactive. When you return to that rhythm, your leadership feels less like a series of reactions and more like a steady cadence. And once you can see yourself clearly, you're ready for the next step in the process: deciding where your energy goes.

People feel your energy before they hear your words, and if you don't choose how you show up, the things you can't control will choose your energy for you. Personal identity answers who you are. Energy answers how you show up, which is where we're headed next.

Core Value Connection

Manageable
Before your day begins tomorrow, take one minute to identify the single emotion or mindset you're bringing into the day. Name it honestly so it doesn't lead you unconsciously. Giving your mindset a name gives you control over how you enter the room rather than letting the moment control you.

Meaningful
Write down one moment from this week when your internal state shaped the way others experienced you. Reflect on what triggered it,

how it affected the interaction, and what it taught you about how your presence influences the people you lead.

Magnetic
Who do I become when I'm not paying attention to what I bring into the room—and who do I want people to experience instead?

CHAPTER 3

Intentional Energy

What you focus on grows—what you ignore fades.

"Where your attention goes, energy flows."
— James Redfield

Most people think their leadership begins when they step into a meeting or start talking to their team. But leadership starts long before anyone else sees you. It starts in the quiet moments before the day picks up speed, when you decide what energy you're going to carry into the spaces that depend on you.

What I've learned, especially on days when everything feels loud and heavy, is that the energy you bring with you isn't random. It's chosen. And if you don't choose it on purpose, something else–email, stress, urgency, someone else's frustration–will choose it for you. Leading on autopilot is not the energy that aligns with **who** you want to be.

One of the most eye-opening moments for me came when I started paying attention to how my day actually began. For years, my mornings followed the same pattern: show up to school, turn on my computer, get a seltzer water, open email, respond to email, sign forms, walk the hallways, connect with people, and get into classrooms. That was my "first eight things." And here's what hit me: only the bottom three—walking hallways, connecting with people, and getting into classrooms, actually gave me energy. Everything else drained it before the day even started.

By the time I reached the things I loved most, I was already in a mindset I didn't want. Email led to more email. A late form led to frustration. A budget question led to worry. And then I'd walk into the hallway carrying that with me. Not because I didn't care, but because I hadn't reset myself before stepping into places where presence mattered.

When I share this with leaders, I show them my list and highlight the ones that fueled me. Every time, you can see the realization wash over people. They start picturing their own mornings. Their own lists and things that need to get done, but when I tell them that if the first thing you do in your day is open email, all you're doing is transferring someone else's to-do list to yours, it starts to hit them that the things they are already starting in a rut.

The real epiphany doesn't happen until I ask them to write down the first eight things they do when they get home, because that's when it hits them: we go home to the people who love us the most and give us the most latitude, and somehow they get the least of us because they love us the most and give us the most latitude. Not on purpose. Not because we don't care, but because we never reset. We never paused long enough to protect the part of us they deserve. Just because someone loves you the most doesn't mean they should get the least of you.

I was scrolling through social media the other day when a clip from *The Office* popped up, the one where a character named Andy Bernard says, "I wish there was a way to know you were in the good old days before you actually left them." I've seen that scene countless times, but the line still catches me. It resonates because so many leaders and educators spend far more time thinking about what's difficult, what's not working, or what's out of their control than they do recognizing what's going well. We focus on the struggle and often miss what's happening right in front of us that is meaningful, healthy, or even really special.

The truth is, what we notice is often a reflection of the energy we bring into the day. That's why that line hits so hard, because the good old days feel impossible to see from the middle of them. Here's the thing we don't always acknowledge: the person most responsible for helping you recognize that you're in the good old days is you. As a leader,

> The truth is, what we notice is often a reflection of the energy we bring into the day.

the energy you bring to the days you are currently in will help them be remembered as the good old days by both you and those you lead. *Your energy doesn't just shape how you experience the day, it shapes how everyone around you experiences it, too.*

When I was a kid, my parents used to tell me, "Don't take these days for granted." I nodded because that's what kids do, but I didn't understand it. Later, when my own children were younger, I heard myself saying the same words to them. And just like I did, they nodded politely without fully grasping what I meant. That's how it goes. The people who are already past the moment see it clearly, while the people in the moment rarely do.

Over the last three years, I've been asked countless times what I miss most about being in a school every day. I don't need more than a second to answer: I miss being part of a team. Not because every day was easy or because everyone always agreed, but because even when things were stressful or frustrating, we knew we were part of something bigger than the moment we were in. *Teams don't just share work, they share energy. And the energy of a healthy team can carry you through moments that would otherwise wear you down.* The small interactions, the in-between moments, the conversations that made you feel seen, those are the things that become the memories you carry forward.

But simply "knowing" you're in the good old days isn't enough. Awareness without action doesn't change anything. Intentional energy is what transforms awareness into action. What matters is how you show up inside those moments—whether you choose to find the joy that exists in the middle of the routine, the stress, the schedule, and the noise. The moments themselves don't transform you; the way you treat those moments does. If all you do is acknowledge that these might be the days you'll talk about someday, but you never slow down enough to appreciate or invest in the interactions that create them, then the awareness doesn't make much difference.

That's where the shift happens. Imagine waking up each morning and intentionally deciding that today, whatever it holds, is part of the good old days. *This is where energy becomes a practice, not an accident.* Not because everything is perfect or smooth, but because the day itself is filled with interactions that matter. Approaching work with that mindset changes the way you enter a room, listen to a colleague, respond to a student, or navigate a tough moment. It nudges you toward being present instead of just busy. It helps you see the value in the things you usually rush past. And while it won't erase the stressors or solve the bigger problems, it absolutely changes the tone and quality of the interactions that shape your day. That's the power of rhythm in leadership, when your internal tempo stays steady, the chaos around you can't throw you off beat as easily.

Those interactions are often the ones that build the memories you later treasure. Twenty years from now, when someone asks what you miss about this chapter of your life, you probably won't talk about the big accomplishments or major milestones. You'll talk about the people. You'll talk about the conversations that mattered, the laughter that cut through a hard day, the moments of connection that reminded you why you chose this work in the first place. If you ever lived in Wisconsin, you'll probably talk about the weather. You'll talk about them because they were the pieces that gave you, and the people you care about, energy. They were the pieces that made the days "good" even when they didn't feel extraordinary at the time. The energy you brought into those moments often determined whether they became memories or missed opportunities.

INTENTIONAL ENERGY

I was recently talking with Dr. Brad Gustafson, best-selling author, Minnesota's Principal of the Year, one of the most grounded people I have ever met, and a leader who has shaped these pages more than he will ever know. We were talking about nostalgia, and he said something that completely reframed it for me. He reminded me that nostalgia isn't just about past moments, it's about the energy we decided to bring to a moment. He laughed and said, "The mere existence of a toy turtle didn't change my life, but in 1987 the energy and possibility wrapped up in my Teenage Mutant Ninja Turtle was nothing short of magical because that's the energy I chose to give to it." Then he added, "If I let four sewer-dwelling turtles change my life for the better, but somehow miss that same energy for the good old days unfolding in my school's hallways, that's on me."

> **The energy you brought into those moments often determined whether they became memories or missed opportunities.**

When we choose to see our days through that lens, to recognize that the good old days aren't just behind us but also right in front of us, it does something powerful. It reminds us to appreciate what we often take for granted. It encourages us to invest in our relationships. It shifts our focus from what's wrong to what's meaningful. *When your energy shifts, your perspective follows.* That's what increases the chances that we'll create more days worth remembering.

This is where intentional energy becomes a leadership skill because of how honestly you look at your habits. We wanted to make sure our staff was connected to the same concept, so we came up with an activity called "My 3." It was essentially about what mattered most to them during the workday. We asked people to name three things that had to happen throughout the day for them to feel successful. The things needed to be something that they controlled. They needed to be manageable, meaningful, and magnetic. Manageable in the scope of their busiest days, meaningful to who they are as a person, and magnetic in that the action could spark more connections to what they are already doing well and enjoyed. It was great because it grounded them in what mattered most. The bonus for us was when we walked into classrooms and left positive notes that matched one of their three, something shifted. We weren't just praising work, we were acknowledging the identity people wanted to bring into their day. Their internal compass became our feedback loop, and the energy of the building changed because we were reinforcing what mattered most to them.

If "My 8" helped me rearrange my day to bring out my best energy, "My 3" helped our staff see their own greatness before the noise of the day drowned it out. These weren't things that we wanted them to do. These were things that they chose, and that we got a chance to acknowledge. I tried to take it one step further and know everyone's 3 at some point in the year. Though I never got to all 60 staff members, I got close, and the process made me better, because not only could I connect to what mattered most to them, I could connect them to other staff members who are working on the same things. The bigger thing for me was that it reduced my leadership drift.

Every leader drifts. It happens quietly. You start the day with good intentions, and then emails stack, conversations pile, meetings run long, and suddenly the version of you that shows up isn't the one you wanted to bring. Drift isn't failure. Drift is forgetting for a moment who you are and what you bring at your best. But the pullback happens through awareness. Drift happens when you fall out of rhythm; awareness is how you find your way back to the beat. When you feel yourself sliding, you pause long enough to ask what you need to reset. For some people, it's a breath. For others, it's a phrase. For others, it's touching the same spot in the building every day, like the "Play Like a Champion Today" sign Notre Dame players hit before they take the field. For me, it was making a thirty-second connection with someone in the building. A call or a text if I couldn't get out of the office. A walk through the hallway outside my office just to find someone to talk to as they walked by. An intentional walk to the kitchen or custodian's room knowing I would find someone in there to connect with. Whatever it is for you, it's personal. It's yours, and it brings you back to yourself.

I had to learn this the hard way more than once. One day I walked into a conversation thinking I was meeting with a few people to clear up a concern. Instead, I walked into a room filled with our entire staff, everyone already seated and ready to let loose. I was frustrated. I felt blindsided. I could feel my whole energy shift in a direction that wasn't going to help anyone. But walking out wasn't an option. So I forced myself to stop reacting to how I got into the room, concentrate on **who** I wanted to be even in a tough moment, and focus on what the people in front of me actually needed from me. Someone to listen to their concerns, even if those concerns were about me. The only way forward was to reset, not pretend, not power through, but reset, and listen long enough to understand their frustration instead of adding my own to the pile. I listened, asked what was one thing that could be done to make it better, and set up a timeline to start working on the issue that they wanted help with right away. They didn't need the issue fixed by the time we left the meeting. They needed assurance that it would be addressed and when I asked about one specific thing that could be done immediately, they knew we would be making progress when they saw it happen right away. When they recognized little wins regarding the specific action, they started believing that things could get better.

That's the difference between reacting and leading. Reacting to the moment would have drained me and everyone in the room. Listening steadied the room and following up made sure that they knew the listening actually happened.

The leaders people trust aren't the ones who are calm by nature. They're the ones who know what steadies them and actually practice it. They create habits that pull them back from drift. They start their day with intention instead of urgency. Their presence doesn't feel perfect, it feels predictable, grounded, and human. The energy they create becomes something people count on, not something people brace for.

Dr. Sanée Bell, Assistant Superintendent of Teaching and Learning in Katy, Texas, has been an award-winning principal, and was featured in Brene Brown's international bestseller, *Dare to Lead*. She is one of the truest leaders I have ever met. She is authentic with her connections, and purposeful in her approach to leadership. In her book, Be *Excellent on Purpose*, Dr. Bell pushes leaders to stop waiting for excellence to happen and instead *choose* it. Her work reminds us that excellence isn't a mood or a motivational poster, it's a discipline of showing up with clarity, conviction, and care. That throughline fits directly into the idea of intentional energy. She argues that the culture you want will never outpace the energy you bring to it, which means leadership begins long before the meeting, the hallway conversation, or the classroom walkthrough. It begins with the decision to bring your best effort on purpose, not by accident and not by convenience.

When you decide, before your feet hit the floor, that you're going to lead with presence instead of passivity, generosity instead of frustration, and purpose instead of autopilot, you give people around you a better chance to rise with you. Bell's message reinforces the idea that leaders don't stumble into excellent cultures; they fuel them.

That's the heart of intentional energy. Choosing what you're going to bring before the world decides for you. Choosing to begin your day with something that fuels you, not something that drains you. Choosing to show up in ways that reflect who you are instead of how fast your inbox fills. And choosing to bring the best of yourself not just to your workplace, but to your home, your people, and the moments that matter when the day is over.

It's not about being flawless; it's about being aware. It's about being present and willing to reset. Being ready to bring yourself back to who you want to be before you take a single step toward the people who rely on you.

> The energy you choose becomes the experience you create.

Because whether it's leadership, parenting, coaching, partnering, teaching, or simply moving through the world with purpose, the idea we all need to keep in mind is that the energy you choose becomes the experience you create.

The more you understand your energy, where it leaks, where it lifts, and how to reset it, the more clearly you begin to see something else: *you can't lead yourself well without a source of internal momentum.* You need something that reminds you why the work matters in the first place. Something that cuts through the noise and reconnects you to purpose. Making someone laugh and smile and think and feel or leaning into a conversation that you know will make you happier when you leave it, or watching a kid run on a playground…whatever it is, the purpose fuels the energy you bring. That is often where joy comes in. Not the big, celebratory kind, but the everyday kind, the moments that refill you before the day has a chance to drain you. Once you start noticing those moments, the work feels different. You feel different. Which brings us to the next part of leading yourself: finding joy in the work.

Core Value Connection

Manageable
Tomorrow, choose one interaction in which you will deliberately shift your energy—slowing down, showing up differently, or pausing before responding. A small, intentional adjustment can alter the tone of an entire moment and create a more supportive environment.

Meaningful
Identify the part of your day when your energy most often drifts. Reflect on what consistently causes that drift and what small adjustment—rest, pacing, boundaries, intention—might bring your attention back in a meaningful way.

Magnetic
If my energy were the only thing people remembered about me today, what story would it tell about who I am?

CHAPTER 4

Finding Joy in the Work

Joy isn't the reward; it's a strategy

*"Joy does not simply happen to us.
We have to choose joy and keep choosing it every day."*
—Henri Nouwen

When I think about joy in the work, my mind always goes back to a single moment on a football field in northern Wisconsin during a graduation ceremony that didn't look anything like the ones we were used to. It was the spring of 2020, and nothing that year felt normal. Schools were shut down. Families were isolated. Traditions were scattered. Large gatherings were banned. And yet we still wanted our seniors to have some kind of celebration, something that let them feel seen, valued, and recognized for everything they had pushed through. The county health department had strict limits. The ceremony had to be outside. Every graduate got a section of the football field that was lined off as a barrier to the next family. Only a limited number of people could be in that section, and because so many people couldn't attend in person, we planned a livestream for families and friends to watch from wherever they were.

We checked everything before people arrived. The audio. The stage. The water. The livestream. All of it. Our team had thought of every detail. But as people started showing up, things started going sideways. The staging area needed to be adjusted. Kids needed more water. And most importantly, the livestream, the one thing we knew people were counting on, stopped working. There was nothing we could do in the moment, and with each minute that passed, my frustration just kept building. It wasn't anger at anyone. It was the helplessness of knowing something meaningful was slipping through our fingers and not being able to fix it fast enough.

I sat in the front row, alternating between watching the kids and checking the texts on my phone. The seniors were doing everything they could to stay present, but I could feel my mind drifting toward everything that wasn't working. I kept trying to push it down and focus on the ceremony, but it felt like the chaos of the moment and the knowledge that I couldn't do anything about it was getting me to a breaking point. It was one of those moments when the rhythm inside me felt out of sync with the rhythm around me and I didn't know what to do.

Then Paige stepped up to the microphone.

She was tiny next to the empty bleachers behind her, standing there in her cap and gown, looking out at a field spread wide with families behind the guise of a white lined barrier. She began talking about her teachers and her friends and the senior drive the town had organized, where the graduates drove through the community and the people lining the streets cheered until their voices cracked. She talked about the kindness people showed. The little things teachers did to stay connected. The way the whole town came together to give the class of 2020 something to hold onto.

And then she said something that made the entire field pause. She said, "Because people are amazing, and that's why I don't hate coronavirus."

There was a collective sigh. I shouldn't have been able to hear it ripple across the football field, but I did. It didn't erase the chaos. But it reframed it. In that moment, the weight we had all been carrying lifted just long enough for people to breathe again. Her words didn't deny the hardship. They didn't pretend everything was fine. They reminded us why we were all trying so hard in the first place, because people matter, and when people matter to you, you keep showing up for them even when the moment is a mess.

For six minutes and sixteen seconds, I wasn't thinking about the livestream or the logistics or everything that was going wrong. I was thinking about what her words represented: her family, her friends, her teachers, her community. All the people who had poured into her. All the people who had built the kind of environment that empowered her to look at one of the hardest moments in her life and still find something good. She was right. People are amazing. Sometimes it takes someone younger than you, standing at a microphone in the middle of an imperfect day, to remind you of that.

What Paige gave us that day was a rhythm reset. A moment that pulled us back to why we were there. A moment that reconnected us and redirected our energy. That single sentence brought us back into alignment.

That moment has stayed with me because it captured something I think we misunderstand about joy. We talk about joy like it's a reward we get after everything is done and the work goes well, like joy waits on the other side of our checklist, ready to show up once the stars align. But joy doesn't show up after things are perfect. Joy shows up when things are meaningful. It appears when our internal rhythm steadies, even while the world around us speeds up, slows down, or stumbles out of tempo. It shows up when we're connected to the people around us and when the work matters enough that

> **Joy shows up when things are meaningful.**

even on the frustrating days, we can still find something that pulls us back toward the good.

A lot of people use the words joy and happiness like they're interchangeable. And honestly, outside of writing this book, I'm never going to stop someone and say, "Well actually…" If someone tells me they're happy at work or joyful at work, my first instinct isn't to correct them, it's to celebrate that something is going right. But inside this leadership work, those two words live in different parts of the house. Happiness is a reaction. It's emotional. It's usually tied to something we don't control. I'm happy when the Packers win. I had absolutely nothing to do with the play calling or the coverage or the route, but in the moment, you'd think I did. And yes, I absolutely believe that sitting in the same spot on the couch wearing the same sweatshirt helps the team in ways science can't fully explain. But the happiness that shows up in that moment is a reaction to something outside of me.

Work has those moments, too. A breakthrough conversation. A great email. A hallway joke that lands perfectly. Those moments give us a lift, but they're not reliable, because the world isn't reliable. Happiness shows up when the conditions are right. Joy is different. Joy is the thing you can choose even when the conditions are not right. Joy is intentional. It's systematic. It's a practice. It's not waiting for something to happen, it's building something that keeps you grounded when the day tilts sideways. Joy is what happens when your intention, connection, and direction fall into a shared rhythm, your rhythm, instead of being pulled into everyone else's.

That's why joy matters so much in leadership. Joy doesn't ask you to pretend everything is great. Joy asks you to stay connected to meaning when things are hard. It keeps you rooted in who you are and why this work matters. Joy is not about the perfect moment, it's about the meaningful one, and meaningful moments can show up even when the livestream is down, the plans are falling apart, and the frustration is real. Joy is the belief that something good can still happen because of the way we show up.

You can build joy the same way you build routines, culture, or habits. You can address them slowly, consistently, and most importantly, with intention. It shows up in how you connect with people. In how you talk to them. In whether you pause long enough to listen. In whether you show up as a human being instead of a job title. Joy is present when people can breathe around you. When they know, they don't have to pretend. When you make it easier for them to show up fully because you're willing to show up fully, too. When joy becomes part of your personal rhythm, people feel it before they hear it, the same way a steady beat changes the whole song.

Everywhere I go I see the same pattern. When joy fades, people don't just lose energy. They lose clarity. They lose curiosity. They lose the sense that what they're doing matters. And when that slips, everything else gets heavier. People shift from showing up with intention to showing up out of obligation. From ownership to compliance. From "I want to be part of this" to "I just need to get through this." When joy disappears, work becomes heavier than it needs to be.

Joy doesn't mean the work is easy. It means the work is connected to something worth doing. It's the difference between dragging yourself through a day and moving through it with purpose. Joy doesn't eliminate frustration. It reframes it. It makes the hard moments survivable because they fit into something bigger. It keeps leaders grounded enough to lead people, not just tasks.

In leadership, joy is a stabilizer. It's the quiet force that keeps you centered when everything around you feels unstable. It's what keeps you from overstating the positive or pretending the negative doesn't exist. Joy is what makes you real in moments when people don't need a polished performance, they need presence. That's why the moment with Paige mattered. It pulled me back into connection. It reminded me that despite everything going wrong around us, something meaningful was happening because of what people had built together.

Organizations that sustain joy don't rely on pep talks. They don't wait for morale boosters. They don't depend on perfect days or flawless systems. They embed joy into the way the work works. They build it into conversations, recognition, the way people treat each other, and into traditions. It's part of how they recover when things go sideways. Joy becomes part of the culture, not an occasional visitor. In healthy organizations, joy isn't a mood, it's a rhythm, and rhythms repeat. They hold. They guide. They keep people moving even when things get tough.

> In healthy organizations, joy isn't a mood, it's a rhythm, and rhythms repeat.

When joy becomes rhythm, the whole environment shifts. People communicate more openly. They recover faster from frustration. They laugh more. They reconnect more. They bring more of themselves to the work because the work gives something meaningful back to them.

The most powerful part of joy in leadership is that it keeps leaders human. It reminds us that leadership isn't a performance, it's a presence. Leadership isn't about being the most positive person in the room as much as it's about being the most grounded one. It's about being real enough that people trust you, steady enough that people feel safe around you, and connected enough that people know they matter.

When leaders choose joy, they make everyone around them better. And they become better in the process. Joy doesn't just influence how leaders feel at work. It shapes who they become while doing the work. It helps them stay anchored in who they are, even when the moment pressures them to be someone else. And when leaders stay anchored, everyone around them feels the difference.

As we move into the next chapter, we shift from energy to clarity. If joy helps you stay rooted in who you are, clarity helps you move toward where you need to go. Joy fuels the work. Clarity focuses it. Both are part of your rhythm and together they allow you to lead from who you are, not from who the moment tries to force you to be.

> It's about being real enough that people trust you, steady enough that people feel safe around you, and connected enough that people know they matter.

Core Value Connection

Manageable
Tomorrow, intentionally notice and name one moment of joy in your day. Capture it—mentally or in writing—so you begin training yourself to recognize what's working instead of only noticing what isn't.

Meaningful
Think about the last time you caught yourself smiling in the work. Reflect on what contributed to that moment and how you might create conditions for similar moments to appear more frequently in your leadership.

Magnetic
If joy became part of my leadership identity, how would that change the way people experience working with me?

CHAPTER 5

Seeing Greatness around You

What you recognize expands

"A person becomes what he praises."
–Johann Wolfgang von Goethe

I was standing in front of a group of principals in Texas when the ordinary became the extraordinary. It wasn't one of those moments where you think, "This is going to be something I talk about for years." It happened quietly, the way most meaningful things tend to happen, tucked inside an ordinary Tuesday during a workshop where we were talking about how to recognize, acknowledge, and extend the great things happening in our schools. I often use the framework as a reminder that meaningful leadership doesn't require nine steps, a graphic organizer, and a color-coded laminated chart. Sometimes it takes ninety seconds and a little courage. I've done it hundreds of times, and this set up to be just like those, until it wasn't.

I asked the room if anyone wanted to share a story about someone on their staff who was doing something great, something small or something big, something for kids, for colleagues, or for the community.

I wasn't looking for perfection. I wasn't even looking for a polished story. I just wanted to hear something real. A principal near the front of the room raised her hand and began talking about a teacher on her staff, we'll call her Angela, who had started a program to collect food for families who needed help on weekends. As she talked, the room shifted. You could hear the pride in her voice. You could feel the respect she had for this teacher. You could see how much she believed in what Angela was doing. There was something in the way she told the story that made it clear Angela wasn't doing this for attention. She did it because she cared, because kids mattered to her, because she saw a need and wouldn't let it sit there unattended.

Like I always do, I recorded the principal telling the story and asked her for Angela's phone number, and sent the clip to Angela so she could see what was being said about her in that room. I also sent the video to the principal so she could forward it to someone in Angela's life outside the school, maybe her spouse, a parent, her friend group, someone who doesn't get to see her impact every day but loves her deeply and would feel proud hearing what she means to her school. I love the activity and it doesn't matter if I have spoken to a group once, twice, or ten times… we are doing the activity as a reminder. The whole thing took ninety seconds. And I thought we were done.

But then, right as we were about to move on, another principal stood up from across the room and said, "Wait, are you talking about this Angela?" She held up a picture on her phone, and it took half a second to realize it was the exact same person. This principal had worked with Angela ten years earlier in a completely different state. Suddenly the room erupted. People laughed. A few gasped. Someone said, "No way!" We took a picture of the two principals and sent it to Angela along with the video.

Twenty minutes later, my phone buzzed. It was a number I didn't recognize…then I realized where it was coming from. It was Angela. Her message was one sentence: "You just made my whole year."

I read her text aloud, and the room let out this collective, emotional sigh, the kind that comes when something true has just landed. I watched the two principals who had talked about her try to hold back tears. I felt it, too. Here's what I know after doing this activity hundreds of times: that moment hits the same way almost every single time. Because deep down, people want to feel seen and people want to see others. We're just moving too fast to slow down long enough to say it out loud. These are the kinds of moments that remind leaders to return to their rhythm, especially in seasons when the speed of the work tries to pull them off center.

That day in Texas taught me something essential about great moments: they almost never walk into a space with a spotlight. They don't announce themselves or ask for attention. They slip quietly in quietly through effort, consistency, and a hundred small decisions most people walk past because they're trying to get to the next thing on their list. The leaders who make the biggest impact aren't the ones waiting for dramatic breakthroughs. They're the ones who notice what's working long before anyone else sees it. They pay attention to effort before results and recognize character before achievement. They see who someone is becoming long before that person can see it themselves. That kind of clarity only comes when a leader's internal rhythm is steady enough not to get thrown off by urgency or distraction.

You can feel this shift every year in schools when the early energy settles and the routines take over. The excitement of the first few weeks gives way to something quieter. The work becomes more patterned. People settle into their own rhythms. And even in the healthiest schools, where people collaborate and check in and share spaces, most adults still spend ninety percent of their day behind a closed door with the group they've been assigned. That's true in all industries. It's no one's fault. It's the nature of the work. But that's when silos start to form, not because anyone wants them, but because the job nudges people into their own corners.

As leaders, I don't know if we can eliminate the silos, but we can absolutely put windows in them. All organizations are filled with amazing things happening all the time. Good cultures recognize those things. Great cultures acknowledge the people responsible for them. But the best culture does something more. It extends the stories. It makes sure the greatness happening in one room doesn't stay trapped inside that room. It travels. It gets shared. It becomes something bigger than the moment or the people who lived it. Extending stories is part of your rhythm. It is the predictable, steady behavior of a leader who refuses to let great work stay small. If you really want to understand why extending stories matters, look at the leaders who make appreciation a cornerstone of their culture. Their work shows that noticing greatness isn't accidental; it's a discipline that changes the way people feel about their work and about each other.

That's where leadership shifts during the routine season. Early in the year, leadership is about personal connection. Once the year settles in, leadership becomes about connecting people to their people. It's making sure individuals don't feel like they're working alone in their own quiet corner. It's helping them feel part of something bigger than their four walls. It's taking the greatness you see and making sure it moves somewhere else.

That's why noticing matters so much. When you see something, say something, and when you say something, say it to someone else, too. Tell the teacher next door. Mention it to someone down the hall. Bring it to a colleague who wasn't in the room. Share it with a spouse or partner or friend. Because when people hear that their work is being talked about beyond the moment, it closes the value gap, the gap between what they do and how they feel

> **When you see something, say something, and when you say something, say it to someone else, too.**

about what they do. It ties their daily work to the people in their life who reinforce their identity and remind them who they are.

You can feel the shift instantly when that gap closes. People walk differently. They stand differently. They carry themselves with more intention because they feel seen in one space and valued in another. Purpose doesn't come from a motivational speech. Purpose is created when someone feels recognized for something that matters and that recognition doesn't stay hidden inside a single room; it gets carried forward.

I saw this come to life during a passing period at our middle school. It was one of those quick stretches of time when the hallways are full of movement and noise. I was standing near a corner when three teachers approached me one after another. Three teachers. Three different stories. Three moments of greatness about three different people. They knew exactly what I was going to do with those stories. They knew I would go find the person being talked about and tell them who said it and what was said. They knew it because someone had done it for them. That's what extension looks like. It connects behaviors and becomes the culture of the building. That is exactly what I saw in that hallway. People recognizing each other. People keeping stories alive. People scanning for greatness instead of problems.

Here's the thing that makes me crazy: people often downplay the very things that make them great. You give someone specific recognition and they wave it off. "Oh, it's nothing." "It's just what I do." Meanwhile, you've watched that same behavior change a kid's day or shift a colleague's confidence or rebuild trust in a family. Leaders need to help people understand that accepting recognition is part of the process. When someone brushes off a compliment, it doesn't just diminish the moment. It discourages the giver from trying again.

I think about a little girl in our elementary school who had gone through more surgeries than most people do in a lifetime. Every day, without fail, I'd see her in the hallway and tell her how beautiful she was and how much she made me smile. And every day she said the same thing: "Thank you," and gave me a smile. No deflection. No "It's not a big deal." No awkwardness. Her gratitude made me want to find her every single day. That is the power of being willing to receive the good someone sees in you. It pulls people back. It strengthens connection. It creates belonging. It creates momentum.

All of this fits inside the truth that greatness isn't hiding. It's happening right in front of us, every day, in every organization, in moments we walk past because we're distracted or tired or thinking about the next thing on our list. People aren't waiting for perfect conditions. They're waiting to be seen. They're waiting for someone to say, "This thing you do, this specific thing…it matters." And the moment you begin to lead this way, something changes in you, too. Your own leadership becomes clearer. You walk into the day looking for things that make people proud of who they are. That is what a personal rhythm does. It keeps you grounded enough to see what matters and calm enough to respond with purpose instead of impulse.

Recognition builds identity. Acknowledgment builds confidence. And when you extend a story to someone who wasn't in the room, it becomes part of the culture. It becomes something people rally around, something they want to be part of. That's what makes this work manageable, meaningful, and magnetic. It doesn't take hours. It doesn't require a committee. It takes a moment. It takes intention. And when you do it consistently, people gravitate toward it. They want to be near leadership that sees them. They want to be near colleagues who recognize them and be in a place where the stories don't stay small.

Seeing greatness early is a discipline. It shifts the environment before any strategy does, and the moment you begin seeing people differently, they begin seeing themselves differently. That's when belonging becomes real.

So the question that carries you into the next chapter is this: Who around you needs to be seen, and what's stopping you from seeing them? Because the moment you start seeing them, everything else begins to change.

> Who around you needs to be seen, and what's stopping you from seeing them?

Core Value Connection

Manageable
Tomorrow, pause once to genuinely notice someone's effort or improvement—without feeling the need to comment on it immediately. The first step in expanding greatness is learning to see what is often overlooked.

Meaningful
Think about the types of greatness you tend to notice first and the types you unintentionally miss. Reflect on what that reveals about your leadership lens and what blind spots you may be ready to adjust.

Magnetic
If I became the kind of leader who consistently noticed greatness early and often, how would that shape the culture around me?

CHAPTER 6

The Pace of Presence

Leading in a way that matches the moment

"Wherever you are, be all there."
—Jim Elliot

I was speaking at an event in my old hometown, and I decided to drive in a little early so I could swing through the neighborhood where I grew up. A lot has changed in that town over the last thirty years, but that block, my block, looked almost exactly the same. Same houses. Same layout. Same feeling. I made one turn and there it was: the house I grew up in. The driveway where fifty kids from my high school once signed their names in spray paint while we decorated a float for homecoming. The lawn I mowed every Saturday. The tree I used to climb and stay in for what felt like hours. The street where we played football until the streetlight came on, which was the universal signal that it was time to go home.

As I slowed the car and took it all in, I thought about how much time I spent right there on that street, in that front yard, backyard, neighbor's yard, bouncing between houses, never once feeling too busy or too overscheduled. My whole childhood lived on that street, and it moved at a pace that allowed me to notice it as it went by.

I feel like leadership changed that pace. The moment I stepped into leading a school, something shifted. I felt like I had to be busy all the time. I felt this pressure—internal, not external—to fill every open space on my calendar. If I had a free block, I'd try to plug it with something. A meeting. A task. A walkthrough. Anything that showed I was "doing." Anything that made it clear I was working hard, staying productive, being a leader who was always in motion.

The strange part is that nobody asked me to operate that way. No one pulled me aside and said, "Hey, make sure your calendar is packed so people know you're earning your role." I created that expectation all by myself. Somewhere along the way, I convinced myself that being visibly busy was the same as being visibly valuable. So, I filled space, not with intention, but with noise. What I didn't realize then was that every unnecessary task I added came with a cost: presence. When leaders hurry, they stop seeing and the people they serve can feel the distance before we ever notice we've created it.

> Somewhere along the way, I convinced myself that being visibly busy was the same as being visibly valuable.

The other issue was that the things I filled my calendar with often took longer than the time I gave them. They spilled into the next block. They added up. They pushed into the parts of my day that actually required my attention. And slowly, I found myself stretched too thin. I was busy, certainly, but not better. I was not present, and I was absolutely exhausted.

Here's the part that took me far too long to understand: busyness feels productive in the moment, but it's often a way of avoiding the parts of leadership that actually require vulnerability. Being present with people means listening, noticing, engaging, supporting, connecting. Busyness lets us hide behind motion, behind emails, behind tasks, behind

THE PACE OF PRESENCE

calendars, because motion can feel safer than moments. Moments require us to show up fully and be human. Tasks sometimes feel easier, because we may have more control over our motion during that time.

Being the busiest doesn't make you the best. In fact, it often pulls you away from the work that matters most. One of the most import-

> **Busyness lets us hide behind motion, behind emails, behind tasks, behind calendars, because motion can feel safer than moments.**

ant responsibilities a leader has is to be present and engaged with people they lead. People don't feel supported by how many tasks you complete. They feel supported by how much you see them, hear them, and understand what their world feels like. They feel supported when you walk with them, not past them. And that tension, between being everywhere and being truly present, is at the heart of what so many leaders wrestle with. Few people speak to that challenge more clearly than Minnesota Principal of the Year and Education Dive's National Principal of the Year, Dr. Jessica Cabeen.

Dr. Cabeen's *Principal in Balance* offers a powerful complement to this idea of presence. Her work reminds leaders that the pace we keep is often the pace we choose, and too often we choose a pace that pulls us away from the people and priorities that matter most. Cabeen argues that leadership becomes unsustainable when our calendars stop reflecting our values, and the result is a version of ourselves who is constantly in motion but rarely in balance. What makes her perspective so meaningful is that she doesn't frame balance as a softer approach to leadership, she frames it as a strategic one. When leaders intentionally align their time with what they say matters, they reclaim the margins where real relationships live.

Her message fits perfectly inside the pace of presence and the rhythm attached to it. Cabeen's work pushes leaders to pause long enough to notice whether their busyness is building something or simply proving something. She challenges us to replace urgency with clarity and to build routines that protect the moments that actually move people forward. In many ways, balance is presence in practice, a deliberate decision to create space for people, not just tasks. It's a reminder that the most effective leaders are not the ones who are everywhere; they are the ones who are fully where they are. Cabeen makes it clear that balance and presence rise together. And when leaders reclaim space in their day, they reclaim the ability to actually see the people they serve.

As kids, presence was automatic. As adults, especially as leaders, presence becomes a choice. This is the personal rhythm at work. It's not about slowing everything down; it's about choosing a pace that allows you to actually be there while the work is happening. When your rhythm is grounded in presence, your leadership stops feeling frantic and starts feeling intentional again. That choice requires attention, and attention requires presence.

Being present makes the people in your space feel like they are the center of your universe. And knowing that alone should give us the motivation to do what we can to be present with them. The people you lead don't need the busiest leader in the building. They need the most present one. They need the leader who knows when to pause, when to see, when to listen, and when to walk slowly enough to notice what's happening right in front of them.

If you work in schools and want to fill your calendar with something that matters, go see kids. Go into classrooms. Go into hallways. In any other leadership role, go into spaces where people are doing the work, learning, trying, growing. Go be where the purpose of the job actually lives.

But—and this part may sting (it did for me)—you don't need to turn every one of those moments into content. The cadence for me was pretty simple. Walk into a room, take a quick picture or video of the room, put the phone away and be present in the room. You may not get the aha

THE PACE OF PRESENCE

moment of the student discovering something they didn't have before and that's OK. You can still get a visual, but more importantly, you get to be present to experience it, and telling that story when you leave is so much more fun. Being present is leadership. The rhythm of presence feels quieter than checking the boxes off to get to the next thing, but it carries you much farther. People feel it long after the moment ends.

Sharing where you are or shining a light on the people you serve isn't the problem; it's the purpose behind it. There's a difference between telling your community what matters and performing your presence for them. There's a difference between documenting learning and turning every interaction into a product. Presence comes first. Reflection comes second. If you reverse the order, you lose the impact, and you risk the authenticity you are trying to display from the Personal Rhythm.

When you show up with that mindset and slow down enough to see what's right in front of you, the work changes. You change. The people around you feel the difference, and so do you. If you really want to fill your calendar with something meaningful, don't fill it with proof that you're working hard, fill it with proof that you're right there with the people who need you.

When people trust your presence, they trust your leadership. Presence builds the kind of connection that makes every room easier to lead, every conversation easier to start, and every relationship easier to strengthen. Presence creates the

> **People move when they feel seen, not when they feel managed.**

conditions that make direction possible, because people move when they feel seen, not when they feel managed.

Because someday—years from now—when someone asks you what you miss most about this chapter of your life, you won't want to talk about your busyness, you'll talk about the impact your presence had on the people you lead.

Core Value Connection

Manageable
Choose one transition point tomorrow—a hallway walk, a meeting entry, or a classroom visit—and deliberately slow your pace for ten seconds to be fully present. Presence sharpens attention and creates steady leadership moments.

Meaningful
Reflect on a recent moment when rushing caused you to miss something important. Consider what would have changed if you had taken a breath and entered more intentionally.

Magnetic
If my presence became my most trusted tool as a leader, how would it transform the moments people have with me?

Summary: The Personal Rhythm

If you strip everything else away—titles, org charts, strategies, initiatives—leadership always comes back to one question: Who are you bringing into the day? Not the version of you on the website biography. Not the version of you in the perfect moment. The one that walks through the door on a Tuesday when the weather is awful, the inbox is full, and your patience is already thin. That's really what this first section has been about. It's the beginning of tuning the personal rhythm you bring into every room.

We've walked through five big ideas, seeing yourself clearly, choosing your energy, finding joy in the work, seeing greatness around you, and matching the pace of your presence to the moment, but they're not five separate pieces. They're one rhythm. A personal rhythm. A way of leading yourself in real time so the person you actually want to be has a better chance of showing up more often.

It starts with the Mirror Test.

The story might be winter in Wisconsin or a federal lawsuit on your doorstep, but the point is the same: you can't lead well if you have no idea which version of yourself is walking into the space. These four simple questions are a way to tap the brakes long enough to be honest with yourself: Who am I right now? Does this reaction reflect my values? Am I responding from my identity or from the stress of the moment? Will people experience consistency or confusion when they walk toward me?

You don't need a nine-step process. You just need a pause. Sometimes you need to take a breath. A moment between the parking lot and the front door, or between the meeting and the phone call, where you check in and ask, "Is this who I want to be right now?" Most of us don't lose our way in the huge moments. Those come with agendas and preparation. We lose our way in the hallway. In the quick reply. In the sigh that lands on someone who didn't deserve it. The Mirror Test gives you a way to catch yourself before those moments turn into your reputation. That simple pause is the reset button in your personal rhythm. Once you start seeing yourself more clearly, you begin to realize something else: your day isn't just happening to you. You're setting it in motion long before anybody else sees you. That's where intentional energy comes in.

When I laid out my "first eight" at work and realized that the only things giving me energy (walking hallways, connecting with people, getting into classrooms) were at the bottom of the list, it explained a lot. It wasn't that I didn't love the people or the work. It was that I had let the structure of my day pull me into a mindset I didn't want before I ever got to the parts that made me feel most like myself. The same thing happened when staff named their "My 3", the three things they needed in a day to feel successful. I wasn't asking them to do more. I was inviting them to notice what filled them up.

Once they could name it, they could look for it. Once I knew it, I could reinforce it. A quick note that said, "I saw you connect with that student you were worried about," suddenly meant more than any generic, "Great job today!" because it was tied to who they wanted to be. Over time, I started to see drift differently. Everyone drifts. You start the day with good intentions and then the emails, conversations, and interruptions pile up. Intentional energy isn't about never drifting; it's about having a way to pull yourself back. A phrase. A doorway. A short

SUMMARY: THE PERSONAL RHYTHM

walk. A 30-second connection in the hallway. Something you do on purpose to remind yourself, "This is who I am. This is how I want to show up," before you step into the next moment.

And once you start pulling yourself back on purpose, you realize you need something deeper than momentum to keep you going when the day gets loud.

You need joy.

Not "everything is awesome" joy or "fake it 'til you make it" joy. The kind of joy we've been talking about here is quieter than that, and stronger. It's not pretending things are fine. It's remembering why the work is worth it even when things are not fine at all. Joy isn't the reward you get after everything works. It's the way you stay human while things are still messy.

It shows up on a football field when the livestream fails and the logistics are falling apart, but a student grabs the microphone and reminds everyone that people are amazing. It shows up when a small act of kindness cuts through a really bad day. It shows up when you're able to laugh, not because the situation is funny, but because you can see the people around you trying their best in the middle of it. Joy keeps you grounded. It keeps leadership from becoming a performance. It restores the rhythm beneath the work so the hard moments don't drown out the meaningful ones. It moves you from "I have to get through this," to "I'm grateful I get to do this," even on the tough days. And once you can see yourself clearly, choose your energy, and stay connected to joy, something else starts to shift in your vision:

You start seeing greatness differently.

The Angela story in Texas brought that to life. Thirty seconds to recognize her in front of her peers. Thirty seconds to acknowledge, with specifics, what she was doing for kids and families. Thirty seconds to extend that story to her and to someone in her world who doesn't get to see her at work. A single text back, "You just made my whole year" was proof of what that moment meant.

But if you look a little deeper, that moment didn't just change Angela's day. It changed the room. It changed the two principals who talked about her. Over time, when you keep doing that, it changes the culture. Once you commit to noticing and naming greatness—Recognize → Acknowledge → Extend—you don't walk the same way through your day. You notice different things. You feel a pull to name what you see. You find yourself telling someone, "I watched the way you handled that conversation," or "I saw how you stayed with that kid," or "I noticed how you made that new person feel like they belonged here." And you don't stop there—you carry the story to someone who wasn't in the room.

Recognition stops being a one-on-one "nice moment" and starts becoming a network of connection. The hallway stories, three teachers telling me three great things about three different people in three minutes, are what culture actually looks like when it's moving. And it does something to you, too. The student who simply said, "thank you" and smiled every time I told her how much she brightened my day made you want to find her over and over again. That's what happens when people let recognition land, it creates a loop. You're more likely to look for greatness when you've felt what happens on the other side of it. By the time you've walked through the chapters, personal identity, energy, joy, and recognition, one more piece of leading yourself comes into focus: Your pace.

> You're more likely to look for greatness when you've felt what happens on the other side of it.

Standing in front of my childhood home, remembering a slower life on that block, made it clear how easy it is for leadership to speed everything up. Somewhere along the way, we start believing that a full calendar is the same as a full life, that being the busiest person in the building means we're the most valuable. So we cram our days, pack our schedules, and unintentionally rush past the very people we're supposed to be leading.

SUMMARY: THE PERSONAL RHYTHM

The problem isn't effort. The problem is misalignment. When your pace doesn't match the moment, people feel it. When you're always hurried, you stop seeing. When every open space gets filled with another task, you stop connecting. When every visit to a classroom becomes content instead of connection, presence turns into performance.

Pace of presence is the part of the rhythm that slows you back down.

It's remembering that people don't need the busiest leader, they need the most present one. They need the leader who can walk into a classroom and actually be there. The one who can stand in a hallway and really listen. The one who can sit in a meeting and give their full attention instead of their leftovers. Presence is what makes the rest of the work possible. When people trust your presence, they trust your leadership.

Put all of that together and you start to see what Part I has been building toward.

This isn't about becoming a perfect version of yourself. It's about building a personal rhythm that gives you a way back to yourself when the day starts to pull you off course:

See yourself clearly.
Decide where your energy goes.
Hold on to joy.
Look for greatness and say it out loud.
Move at a pace that lets people feel your presence, not just see your name on their calendar.

You won't nail all five every day. None of us do. There will be days when the cold wins, the email gets to you, the meeting goes sideways, or you walk past a great moment without saying anything. That's part of the deal.

But now you have a way back. You have questions that pull you out of autopilot. You have habits that can reset your energy before you walk through a door. You have stories that remind you joy is still possible in the middle of the mess. You have a lens that helps you see and share greatness so people feel seen. You have a pace that lets your presence match the moment.

That's what Part I has been building: not a polished version of you, but a grounded one. A leader whose presence feels steady, human, and intentional. Someone people know they can count on, even on the days when the circumstances are anything but ideal.

Because this first section isn't just about strategy; it's about the personal rhythm of your leadership, how you treat yourself and the people around you when no one is scripting the moment. And once that rhythm is in place, you're ready for the next layer of the work: Taking that identity into the spaces you enter and learning how to lead people with that in mind.

PART II

The People Rhythm

*Connection:
Building Trust and Collaboration*

CHAPTER 7

Presence Over Position

Influence without authority

"A boss has the title, a leader has the people."
—Simon Sinek

I wasn't in the school kitchen for more than three minutes before I could feel something wasn't landing the way I intended. I had stopped in on my way to a meeting just to say hi, check in, and see how people were doing. Nothing formal, nothing evaluative, nothing official. I didn't have a clipboard or a list of things to observe. I just wanted to show up and be present for a moment. I talked to the staff as they were on their break between serving breakfast and getting ready for the lunch rush. The food service director was picking up milk slips from classrooms so it was just me and the staff. About an hour later, the food service director walked into my office and asked if everything was OK. When I told her yes, everything was fine, she said the staff thought I was looking for her and was worried because I had stopped by. That hit me harder than I expected. A visit that I thought was casual and friendly had landed as a warning to them. A moment I intended as connection was interpreted as concern. It wasn't anything I had said or done. It was what my presence implied based on the pattern of when I usually showed up, and more importantly, when I didn't.

The truth was, I spent a lot of time walking hallways and popping into classrooms, but I did it when it fit the rhythm of my own day. The kitchen ran on a completely different clock. Half the staff left after the break between breakfast and lunch. Some of the remaining staff left after lunch was served, and a few stayed to clean the kitchen and prep the next day. The times I normally walked the building didn't line up with the times the kitchen was fully staffed. So when I appeared in their space during the break when everyone was still there, it meant something to them, even if it was unintentional to me. It was a good reminder that people experience us before they hear us, and that their interpretation of our presence is shaped by the history they have—or don't have—with us. That moment in the kitchen pushed me to look more closely at how often leaders underestimate the impact of their presence and how often people fill in gaps based on incomplete information.

I've come back to the idea many times that our actions set the standard, and our silence sets the boundaries. But through conversations with leaders all over the country, I've realized the real issue isn't silence itself, it's the perception of silence. In every organization, things happen behind closed doors that absolutely should stay behind closed doors. Tough conversations, accountability, coaching, and conflict resolution all live in private spaces for good reasons. The problem is that everyone else only sees the before and after, not the middle. They don't see the conversation you had in your office. They don't see the context, the coaching, or the follow through. So they fill in the blanks with whatever story makes sense to them at the time. When they haven't interacted with you enough to know your patterns, the story they create may be nowhere near reality.

That's where presence becomes so critical. It isn't because presence solves every problem. It's because presence builds the pattern people fall back on when they don't have all the information. When people have experienced you as consistent, accessible, grounded, and human, they interpret the things they can't see through that lens. They give you the benefit of the doubt. They assume positive intent. They trust that you're addressing things even if they didn't witness the process themselves. When relationships get there first, the role doesn't have to do all the heavy lifting.

The opposite is also true. When people rarely see you, or only see you when something is wrong, uncertainty grows. Doubt grows. The story grows on its own. And that's how a two-minute stop in the kitchen turns into worries about whether something is wrong. It wasn't that the staff misread me. It was that I hadn't given them enough experiences of me to read anything else. That's the part of leadership we often forget. It's not the big moments that shape trust, it's the accumulation of small, human interactions that seem insignificant in the moment but add up over time. We never want to miss something in the big moments, but the social capital we build in the small moments gives us a little latitude if we need it in those big moments.

The more I've reflected on this, the more I've realized how often leaders confuse presence with personality. Presence isn't charisma. It isn't confidence. It isn't being the loudest or most dynamic person in the room. Presence is a practice. It's the habit of showing up on purpose. It's the choice to breathe instead of rush, to pause instead of react, to enter a space with curiosity instead of tension. People read our nonverbals long before they process our words. The way we walk in, the expression on our face, the tone we naturally carry, the pace we're moving, those things set the temperature of the room before we ever get to clarify our intentions. If people don't know us well, they default to interpreting those cues through the lens of the position, not the person.

That's why the work of leading yourself—everything from understanding your intention, to managing your energy, to finding joy in the moments that matter—shows up so loudly in the People Rhythm. You don't build presence in the moment you need it. You build it in every moment leading up to that moment. The quick hallway conversations, the sincere check-ins, the times when you stop and truly listen, the rhythm of how you move through the building, those things form the storyline people attach to you. And whether leaders realize it, people are reading that storyline every time you enter a room.

A lot of people try to wiggle out of this by saying they don't have influence. But everyone in the room influences the room. Some people lift it. Some steady it. Some quiet it. Some drain it. Influence isn't optional; it's happening whether you claim it or not. The only real question is whether you're influencing the room on purpose or by accident. If that thought makes you nervous, here's the reassuring part: *influence is built on patterns, and patterns can be changed.* You can decide how you show up. You can decide which rhythms you want to create. You can decide the story people will eventually attach to you. The best part of presence is that it's not fixed, it's shaped moment by moment.

> But everyone in the room influences the room.

Looking back on that kitchen moment, I don't think the staff was wrong to wonder why I was there. Their reaction was simply the natural result of the limited pattern I had created. Once I adjusted my routine, showed up at different times, spent time in the kitchen consistently instead of occasionally, had actual conversations instead of quick waves, things changed. That change didn't come because I explained myself, but because I showed myself. That's the part leaders underestimate. You don't *tell* people who you are. You *show* them, repeatedly, until the pattern becomes clear enough that they trust it.

The People Rhythm has very little to do with controlling the room. It has everything to do with shaping how people experience you so that when you walk in, they don't brace; they settle. They don't assume the worst, they assume the pattern they've already come to know. The moment your presence shifts from being interpreted through your title to being understood through your identity, your influence becomes something people welcome.

Presence isn't about entering a room with authority. Presence is about entering a room with clarity about who you are and how you want people to feel when you arrive. It's the bridge between leading yourself and leading others. It's the moment when your identity becomes visible, when your values become felt, and when your consistency becomes the reason people trust you. The more intentional about who you are when you walk into the room, the more influence you'll have once you're in it.

Core Value Connection

Manageable
Tomorrow, choose one moment to lead with presence instead of position: pause before offering direction and make eye contact with the person in front of you. Don't correct, fix, advise, or redirect first. Simply signal, "I'm here with you." This shift builds relational safety before any leadership move.

Meaningful
Recall a moment when someone's presence influenced you more than their title. Think about what qualities made that presence meaningful and how those same qualities could shape your own leadership.

Magnetic
If people followed me because of who I am rather than the position I hold, what would need to become more consistent in my interactions?

CHAPTER 8

Checking In With VS. Checking Up On

Leading through care, not compliance

"Leaders who don't listen will eventually be surrounded by people who have nothing to say."
—Andy Stanley

Imagine this: it's Friday the 13th, five degrees outside, a full moon is hanging in the sky, and it is exactly one week away from a holiday break. If you've ever worked in a school on a day when even one of those things is in play, you already know the kind of energy it creates. If you haven't, I encourage you to sub on a day when one thing is off. And if you really want to understand the full impact, I double-dog dare you to sub on a day when they all combine. People talk about the weather, the moon cycle, the calendar, and the countdown to break like they're jokes, but the truth is that these things stack together and shift the entire emotional temperature of a building. You can feel it in the parking lot before you ever walk inside.

Days like that have their own weather system. The energy is higher, the patience is thinner, the little things feel bigger, and the adults are doing everything they can to keep the emotional walls standing, not just for students but for themselves. These are the days when you can walk into a classroom and immediately understand that everyone, kids and adults, is running on a slightly different wavelength. They're showing up. They're doing the work. But they're carrying more than what you see.

That's one of the things we forget most easily in leadership. We walk into classrooms and offices and meetings and see people doing their jobs. What we don't see is everything they had to push through before they arrived. Maybe they were up with a sick child. Maybe they're worried about a family member. Maybe they fought traffic, forgot the food they were bringing to the potluck, or got a difficult email before they ever walked into the building. Maybe something in their world feels heavier than they're ready to carry that day. The point isn't to assume what people are dealing with. The point is to remember they're dealing with something. When you hold that as part of your leadership lens, it changes the way you walk into conversations. You give people a little more room. You ask questions instead of assuming motives. You listen more closely. You slow yourself down before responding. And when you do that, people walk out of those conversations feeling different. They feel supported, not judged. They feel understood, not managed. They feel seen, not just for their work, but for their humanity.

This is the People Rhythm in action. It's the steady, intentional way leaders show up for others over time, not just in moments of evaluation or crisis. When your rhythm with people is grounded in empathy and consistency, your presence stops feeling transactional and starts feeling trustworthy.

As I thought about days like that in schools, I kept coming back to the difference between *checking up* on people and *checking in* with them. Leaders talk a lot about micromanagement, usually in the context of insisting, "I'm not one of those leaders." But the more leaders I talk with, the more I realize people end up micromanaging without

CHECKING IN WITH VS. CHECKING UP ON

knowing they're doing it, not because they want to control others, but because they misunderstand the impact of their presence. Checking up on people feels judgmental. Checking in with people feels supportive. Those two experiences are completely different, even when the leader's intention is the same.

What often separates them is something as simple as frequency and content, how often you show up and what you talk about when you do. If the only time you walk into someone's space is to talk about data or deadlines or accountability measures or initiatives, then your presence becomes tied to pressure whether you want it to or not. It doesn't matter if your tone is friendly or your intentions are good. If the timing and the topic always line up with pressure, the message people receive is, "I'm here to see whether you're doing the thing." That is checking up on.

But when you show up consistently, long before anything is due or urgent, your presence feels completely different. When your conversations include how people are doing, what they're learning about their kids, what they're proud of, what they want support with, or how the process is going rather than how the result landed, you're checking in with. That's when your presence becomes familiar. That's when it feels human again. And that's when people stop bracing themselves every time you walk into a room.

A quick audit of any leader's week tells you almost immediately how people are experiencing you. Where did you spend your time? Who did you spend it with? What were you talking about when you were there? The answers don't lie. They show you who feels supported and who feels evaluated. They show you who sees you regularly and who only sees you when something is wrong. They reveal a deeper truth leaders sometimes overlook: frequency builds familiarity, and familiarity builds trust. People don't need you to fix everything. They need to know you'll show up before everything falls apart.

I see this all the time at the beginning of the school year. I have been so lucky to help welcome staff back to schools all over the country.

Some events are huge, others are small. Some have pomp and circumstance, others we are trying to find a way to get the projector working. All have two things in common. First, it's my favorite time of the year, by far. The excitement in large venues and small rural villages are the same…the excitement is palpable. The other thing almost every welcome back has is that moment when someone gets up in front of the staff and starts to thank specific groups for the work they have done to get the buildings ready. The custodians, kitchen staff, bus drivers, and anyone else who played a role behind the scenes. After the event I try to find the person that made the announcement, who is usually the superintendent or board president, and ask the question (away from everyone else, always), "When is the second thank you?" Because if the second thank you doesn't happen until their designated appreciation week, we've lost all the momentum, and I know this because I did it more often than I care to admit. The change came with a simple behavior. Adding two employee groups to a shared administrative calendar on the Mondays of each week was a reminder to spend a little more time in that area during that week. It didn't solve all the issues, but it kept me accountable to the groups, and to my administrative team.

As the year settles in and the initial excitement fades, routines begin to take over. Routines are the backbone of a school. They ground people. They stabilize the work. But routines also have a way of isolating people if leaders aren't paying attention. If we only show up when someone is struggling, that's not support, it's triage. It's crisis management dressed up as care. And by the time we arrive, everything we say sounds like checking up on, not checking in with, no matter how gently we try to say it. People don't remember our intentions in those moments. They remember when we came.

> If we only show up when someone is struggling, that's not support, it's triage.

CHECKING IN WITH VS. CHECKING UP ON

But when we start checking in early with simple, casual, human conversations, it is less likely that people get to that breaking point. But even if they do, they know they have been supported along the way because they don't feel like they're carrying the load alone. They don't feel like problems quietly built up until they couldn't handle them anymore. They don't feel like our presence is a signal that something has gone wrong. They feel like we've been with them along the way, not arriving after the fact. That idea isn't abstract. It's been lived, tested, and proven in real schools by leaders who understood that presence, not pressure, changes culture.

One of the most powerful real-world applications of People Rhythm comes from the work of NAESP Virginia Principal of the Year Hamish Brewer, whose turnaround of Fred Lynn Middle School is as inspiring as it is instructive. When Brewer arrived as principal in 2017, the school was facing chronic disengagement, low morale, and academic struggles—and had lost its accreditation. He brought with him not just leadership expertise, but an ethos rooted in relentless belief in every child and every adult in the building.

A single initiative or program didn't drive Fred Lynn's turnaround. It came from embedding a relentless presence and a purposeful culture into the school's daily life. From murals that reflected student identity to beginning each day with announcements reminding students they were loved and valued, Brewer made connections visible and unavoidable. His leadership was centered on checking in with people—students and staff—every single day, long before issues surfaced or data demanded attention.

His approach focused on elevating the voice, building community through shared traditions, and reinforcing a simple, yet powerful, message: *Everyone belongs and everyone matters.* By showing up consistently, listening deeply, and engaging early rather than only when problems arose, Brewer created a rhythm that felt human rather than hierarchical. Through intentional structures and symbolic practices that emphasized support over judgment, he helped shift the school's culture toward trust, engagement, and collective responsibility—transforming a struggling school into a thriving, fully accredited one in just eighteen months.

Watching leadership like that in action forced me to reflect on my own seasons as a leader—and the difference between when I checked in early and when I showed up too late. The more I think about my best leadership seasons, it's easy to see that I was at my best when I checked in early, not checked up late. When people saw me long before anything went wrong. When my presence wasn't tied to pressure but to partnership. I was at my worst when I felt like I had to buy them pizza to show up in their space. Everyone loves pizza. But pizza isn't a relationship builder. Pizza is a celebration. Conversation is the connection, and it's the conversation that does the heavy lifting.

All this connects back to that morning with the full moon, the freezing air, and the countdown to break. Days like that remind us of something simple, but essential: We may not know exactly what everyone is going through, but we do need to know they're going through something. When you enter conversations with that in mind, you listen differently. You don't rush. You don't assume. You don't "check up on" someone who's barely holding it together. You walk in with empathy in the front of your mind. You check in with them and give them room to breathe. It's in that breathing room, where people regroup, reset, and return to the work with more clarity and more capacity than they had before.

> **We may not know exactly what everyone is going through, but we do need to know they're going through something.**

All organizations are full of external factors we can't control. The weather, the calendar, the moon phases, the community noise, the personal challenges, none of it cares about our plans. It all comes together in unpredictable ways, and the adults in the building adapt as best they can. Recognizing that reality doesn't make you soft as a leader. It makes you steady and gives you the awareness needed to show up for people in ways that build trust instead of tension. It shifts your lens from accountability to humanity. When people trust your presence, they trust your feedback, your decisions, and your leadership.

At the heart of it all, *leadership is about how we show up*. On the days when everything feels off, people don't need speeches or fixes or perfectly-structured support plans. They need someone who listens more and talks less. Someone who sees their effort, even when the result isn't perfect. Someone who checks in with them before the weight gets too heavy. Someone who remembers that behind every role is a person doing the best they can with everything they've brought into the day.

When leaders show up with that awareness, when they check in early, check in often, and check in with empathy, people walk out of conversations feeling steadier than when they walked in. They feel like they're not carrying everything alone. They feel like the walls they're holding up don't rest entirely on their shoulders. That feeling makes the work better and the culture stronger. It gives people something they don't always get on the difficult days: a reason to believe they're going to get through it, because someone is walking with them, not checking on them.

Core Value Connection

Manageable
Tomorrow, send one short message or make one brief stop simply to check in—with no request, no reminder, and no task attached. Genuine connection deepens trust because it's not tied to compliance.

Meaningful
Think about someone you supervise or support. Reflect on the signals—intended or not—that your recent interactions have sent about whether you trust them to do the work without oversight.

Magnetic
If people felt genuinely supported rather than monitored, how would that change the way they show up in their work?

CHAPTER 9

The Candy Hearts

The small signals that shape big perceptions

"Attention is the rarest and purest form of generosity."
—Simone Weil

Valentine's Day always brings a certain energy into schools. The cards, the candy, the excited kids, it's a season that shows up in every building, every year. During one of those stretches, I was scrolling through Instagram or TikTok and came across a video imagining what it would look like if school administrators made candy hearts for their staff. Each little pastel heart had leadership messages printed on them: Remember Your Why. Build Relationships. Do It for the Kids. Be Intentional.

I laughed, but I also realized how often I had relied on those same kinds of sayings over the years, tossing them into conversations or meetings without giving people any real context for what they meant or how to apply them. I may have had every motivational poster created in my office at some point. They evoked emotion and when I started leading, I thought that's what people needed most. It's also where I've gotten myself into trouble. Not because the statements are wrong–they can be powerful—but because without a clear understanding of the process behind them, they become phrases people hear rather than practices people live.

That's where the "red car theory" comes in. If I asked you how many red cars you saw on your way to work last week, you probably couldn't tell me because you weren't paying attention to them. But if I offered you a thousand dollars for every red car you saw on your way to work next week, you would suddenly notice red cars everywhere. You would be looking for them with purpose, tuned in to something that wasn't even on your radar before. That's what intentionality really is: focused awareness with a purpose behind it.

That focus disappears quickly if leaders overload the message. If I told our staff, "I'll give you a thousand dollars for every red car you see on your way to work next week," and then added, "But I also need you to document what type of car it was, how many people were inside, and the exact mile marker where you saw it," the whole process becomes overwhelming. Even if someone tried to do it, the mental load would eclipse the benefit. The task that started simple and motivating would become overwhelming. That's what happens when leaders attach so many layers to a concept that the purpose gets lost in the process.

The more I paid attention, the more I realized that leadership tends to fall apart at both ends of the spectrum. It's almost a Three Bears situation: too hot, too cold, and somewhere in the middle is where the real work actually happens. On one end, leaders hand out the catchy phrases without any substance behind them. "Be intentional" becomes a poster. "Build relationships" becomes a slide in a presentation. "Work smarter, not harder" becomes a well-meaning nudge with no direction attached. The phrases look good, they sound good, they feel good in the moment, but they change nothing because people don't know what to do with them.

On the opposite end, leaders take a simple idea and bury it under layers of documentation, metrics, tracking systems, and expectations

THE CANDY HEARTS

that stretch a manageable concept into something heavy. Suddenly, the phrase loses the energy that made it motivating in the first place. The clarity gets swallowed by complexity. The spirit of the message gets lost in the requirements attached to it. People aren't inspired; they're frustrated by the details.

And somewhere between the empty slogan and the exhausting system is the place where leadership actually lives: the meaningful middle. This middle ground is where rhythm begins to matter. It's the difference between leadership that spikes in moments and leadership that people can feel consistently over time. That's where a phrase becomes more than words but less than a burden. It's where leaders provide enough clarity for people to start and enough purpose for them to keep going. It's where the message has context without becoming complicated, and direction without becoming rigid. It's where people understand what to pay attention to and why it matters, but still feel supported enough to bring their own skill, judgment, and humanity into the work.

The middle is where phrases become practices, repeated often enough to become the rhythm of how people experience leadership. Manageable is where the work stays doable instead of draining. Meaningful is where people can see both the purpose and the path. That's why leadership language can't live at the extremes. Too little direction and it becomes noise. Too much direction and it becomes pressure. But when leaders anchor their message in purpose, clarity, and lived behavior, it becomes something far more powerful, something people can actually feel and follow.

The candy heart clichés aren't inherently flawed. They just can't stand alone. The statements become meaningful when we help people understand what to pay attention to, how to focus their energy, and what success looks like in context. Without that, it's just a phrase leaders repeat because it sounds good. But with the right clarity behind it, they become tools that shape how people show up, how they engage, and how they spend their time.

The truth is, people don't need more catchy sayings. They need meaning. They need direction. They need to understand how a concept fits into their daily work in a way that feels manageable and purposeful. That's when they start to matter.

> **The truth is, people don't need more catchy sayings. They need meaning.**

Not when it's written on a candy heart or tossed out in a meeting, but when it's tied to a clear purpose and practiced consistently. Intentionality, on its own, won't change everything. But being intentional about what matters most is where the real change begins.

Core Value Connection

Manageable
Tomorrow, offer one small, sincere signal of appreciation—something quick, specific, and unexpected—to someone who wouldn't see it coming. Small signals shape big perceptions.

Meaningful
Reflect on a time when a tiny gesture meant more to you than a major recognition. Consider why it mattered and what it revealed about your own need to feel seen.

Magnetic
If small, sincere signals became a defining feature of our culture, how would people describe working here?

CHAPTER 10

Everyone's Favorite

Why consistency matters more than charisma

"Long-term consistency beats short-term intensity."
—Bruce Lee

I love speaking to groups. I absolutely love the energy and the engagement and knowing that if they take one thing back with them, they will get more momentum and be happier in a job that often feels isolating. When I get home from events, I tend to crash. Exhausted for the right reasons, but still, exhausted. One day after making it home from an event, I got an email from someone who had attended a keynote on that particular day. This person was upset about a story I told during the presentation, a story I've told hundreds of times over the last ten years. In all that time, I had never once received a negative reaction to it. So when this email arrived, I was shocked, but immediately gave the person credit for reaching out. It takes courage to write something like that. It's uncomfortable and vulnerable, and it's much easier to say nothing and simply walk away holding your own interpretation. This person didn't do that, and I respected it.

But the irony was impossible to ignore. Earlier that same day, I received another email from someone who attended the exact same keynote. Same room, same stories, same delivery. That person said the presentation meant a great deal to them, specifically referencing the exact moment the first person was upset about. One story, two completely different responses.

What lingered with me even more than the feedback was my reaction to the two messages. When the positive email came in, I responded immediately. I thanked the person, expressed my appreciation, and moved on with my day. It added a nice moment to the morning, and then life continued. But the negative email grabbed me differently. I must have read it at least ten times, trying to understand exactly what the person meant. I replayed the moment in my head. I questioned my delivery, my tone, and even my intention. I drafted and redrafted my response before finally sending a simple thank-you, apology that the person felt this way, and acknowledgment for their willingness to reach out. Even after replying, that email traveled with me into the rest of the evening. I was quieter. I was less present. I was still thinking about it long after everyone else had moved on.

It's astonishing how quickly one moment can pull you out of the room you're actually in. Leaders know this feeling better than most. We pour ourselves into the work, into planning, into preparation, into clarity of message. We walk into rooms hoping to connect, to encourage, to support, to stretch people toward something better. When ninety-nine people nod, smile, or engage, it feels good. But when one person doesn't? When one person reacts differently than we expected? That's the moment that tends to stick in our heads.

The uncomfortable truth is that the negative voice almost always initially feels louder than the supportive one. Not because it's more accurate. Not because it's more representative. But because leaders care. Leaders

> **The negative voice almost always initially feels louder than the supportive one.**

want to get it right. Leaders want the work to matter. When you care deeply, even gentle criticism feels sharper. Even a small misunderstanding feels heavier, and even when the vast majority of people are with you, it's easy to let your mind orbit the one person who isn't.

It reminded me of something every leader eventually confronts, no matter how long they've been doing the work: you are not going to be everyone's favorite. You can be thoughtful, prepared, caring, consistent, and intentional, and still someone in the room may not connect with you. It is part of the work, part of the responsibility, and part of the emotional weight that comes with leading people.

Yet even knowing that, the truth still stings a little. Leaders are human. We're wired for connection and want to do right by people. Because we care so deeply, it is easy to fall into the pattern of giving more attention to the one person who didn't connect than the many people who did. We replay the moment and rewrite our words in our minds. We wonder if we should have said something differently or carry it long after everyone else has forgotten it.

Here's the thing, though: *the more time you spend thinking about not being everyone's favorite, the less time you have to actually be someone's.* When you allow one difficult reaction to consume you, you tend to lose sight of the people who are moved, supported, encouraged, or inspired by what you do. You miss the impact that is actually happening because you're too focused on the approval you didn't receive.

Everyone who works with kids has a chance to be the one that those kids tell their own kids about someday. Anyone who leads adults has the chance to be the person that someone tells a story about at a dinner table or on the way to a game. You may not be everyone's favorite, but you will be someone's. When leaders carry that truth with them, it changes the way they show up. It creates a steadiness and clarity that shifts us from worrying about acceptance to focusing on purpose.

That shift, from approval to purpose, is one of the most important emotional transitions a leader can make. Approval is external. It depends on the mood of the room, the experiences people bring with them, the expectations they hold, and the stories they've lived before you ever walked in the door. Purpose is internal. It's grounded. It's steady. It's the part of leadership that doesn't wobble when the feedback arrives differently than you hoped. It brings you back to the Personal Rhythm, who you are at your best.

Leading from purpose doesn't mean you ignore feedback. It doesn't mean you stop caring about people's experiences or perspectives. It simply means you don't let a single moment rewrite your identity or shrink your presence for everyone else. It gives you the emotional space to absorb the hard moment without letting it define you.

The other thing that I thought about after I had a chance to pull back from the emails was that people react through the lens of their own stories, not yours. The exact same moment can land as healing for one person and hurtful for another depending on their past experiences, what they walked in carrying, or what they hoped to hear. Sometimes people love what you say because it speaks directly to their story. Sometimes people struggle with what you say because it speaks directly to their story. Neither reaction makes you good or bad. It simply means you are speaking to a room full of humans, each carrying their own world into the space.

Understanding that changes the way you approach things. It makes feedback feel less personal and more contextual. It helps you hold the criticism without letting it hold you. It helped me see that leadership isn't about controlling people's reactions, it's about staying grounded in who I was while honoring how others experienced me.

Here's where the People Rhythm comes in as the heartbeat of connection, trust, and emotional steadiness in leadership. The People Rhythm isn't just about how you treat others; it's also about how you treat yourself. When leaders don't understand this rhythm, moments like that email become heavier than they need to be. When they do understand it, those same moments become guideposts instead of roadblocks.

Leaders who live in the People Rhythm know that connection doesn't require universal approval. It requires authenticity. It requires presence. It requires consistency. People don't need their leader to be flawless. They need their leader to be human. They need them strong enough to stay steady, and grounded enough to hold many perspectives without collapsing under them.

When you lead from that place, something meaningful shifts. You stop chasing the version of yourself you think every person wants, and you start becoming the version people actually need. You stop keeping emotional score based on who approved and who didn't. You stop shrinking because one person felt differently. You stop letting the single voice at the edge of the room drown out the dozens at the center.

> **You stop chasing the version of yourself you think every person wants, and you start becoming the version people actually need.**

That's when leadership becomes a little lighter, but more importantly, that's when your steps become steadier. That's when your presence becomes clearer, not because everyone loves you, but because you're no longer trying to earn something that can't be earned in the first place.

Leadership becomes infinitely more human once you stop expecting emotional perfection from yourself. You are allowed to be affected by criticism. You are allowed to have a moment where something lands differently than you expected. What matters is that you don't let that reaction redefine your purpose or shrink your presence for the people who still need you. I am going to read that paragraph over and over until it starts to sink in, because I know it is one of the things I struggle with the most, as many leaders do.

Don't ever forget that someone is watching you and learning from you. Not in a creepy CIA-checking-your-phone kind of way, but they are watching what you do and learning from how you interact. Someone is quietly grateful for you in ways they may never express. Someone walks into their classroom differently because of something you said. Someone feels more capable, more grounded, or more hopeful because of you. None of that changes because one person experienced you differently.

You're not going to be everyone's favorite, but you are absolutely going to be someone's. When you lean into that, when you choose to lead for the impact rather than the approval, you end up mattering to far more people than you ever expected.

Core Value Connection

Manageable
Tomorrow, choose one behavior—tone, punctuality, follow-through, or attitude—and deliver it consistently in every interaction, regardless of the situation. Consistency is often more powerful than charisma.

Meaningful
Identify a leader you trust because of their consistency. Reflect on the habits they demonstrate that make them dependable and how you might model those same behaviors.

Magnetic
If my consistency became the reason people trusted me, what story would it tell about who I am as a leader?

CHAPTER 11

Build Back Relationships

Repairing trust begins one intentional moment at a time

"The real test of leadership is not how you handle agreement, but how you repair connection after disagreement."
—Peter Drucker

When I was in elementary school, my principal's name was Mr. Bright. He walked the halls every day, stopping into classrooms, checking in on kids, offering a smile, a wave, or a quick hello. He was one of those principals who was simply there, and for the most part, I liked him a lot. There was something steady about him, nothing flashy, nothing forced, just a quiet consistency that made him feel like part of the daily rhythm of the building. The kind of presence you don't fully appreciate as a kid because it seems so normal, but later realize was anything but.

Until the day I decided it would be funny to call him "Not-So-Bright" in front of my class. It wasn't clever. It wasn't kind. It wasn't even original. But I was a kid who liked being on stage, and I convinced myself that the comment would get a laugh. I liked getting reactions. I liked the attention. I liked the feeling of "knowing the room," even though in that moment I clearly didn't. So I said it—loud enough for him and all my classmates to hear.

And of course, once one kid goes for the joke, other kids follow. They laughed. A few repeated it. Someone whispered it again just to see if they'd get the same reaction. The moment snowballed quickly, and the air in the room shifted from playful to uncomfortable. What felt funny in my head felt different in the air. I knew instantly that I had crossed a line.

I got called to the office. My mom got called. There were consequences. The whole thing unfolded exactly the way you'd expect when an elementary kid tries to score points with peers at the expense of an adult. What I remember most is that the walk to the office felt longer than usual, like the hallway itself stretched on purpose to make me think harder about what I'd done. When I got there, the secretary stared at me while I waited and I remember thinking, *I wonder if she laughed or if she now considered me to be a bad kid*. It was not a great experience.

A few decades later—yes, decades—I was back in my hometown one summer and drove by my elementary school. I noticed the school doors were open. It was the time of year when only a few people were in the school and the custodians were getting the rooms ready and the floors cleaned. I decided to walk inside and just look around. I smiled when I passed Mrs. Schustad's first grade classroom, almost gagged when I walked by Mr. Krief's fifth grade room, where the only thing I remember was dissecting a frog. As I made the loop around the building and headed toward the exit, the office was right in front of me, and it all came back. It's funny how our bodies remember things long after our minds try to move on. I walked past that doorway as an adult, a grown man, a principal turned superintendent, and still felt a shadow of that eleven-year-old kid who made a bad decision trying to be funny.

BUILD BACK RELATIONSHIPS

Something else happened after that moment when I was in elementary school. Something I didn't fully understand until years later when I became a principal myself, and honestly didn't fully grasp until I was walking through the hallways that summer.

Before the incident, I saw Mr. Bright regularly, but not constantly. He popped into classrooms and said hello in the hallways. But after the incident, it felt like I saw him everywhere. He appeared in the lunchroom, the hallway, the library, and even during recess. Not in a hovering or disciplinary way, he wasn't checking up on me or waiting for me to mess up again. He was checking in with me. Genuinely talking to me. Asking questions. Connecting. Being kind. Most importantly, smiling. Knowing what I know now, it was clear he was intentionally placing himself in spaces where we would interact. Not to remind me of the mistake, but to make sure that moment wasn't the only thing between us. We had a negative interaction, and he refused to let that define our relationship. He wanted to build it back. That's the People Rhythm at work. It's the steady choice to show up again after a moment of tension, not to erase what happened, but to make sure it doesn't become the only thing that defines the relationship.

In schools, and in any organization, there will always be tough conversations. Conversations about performance, behavior, expectations, or accountability. Conversations that weigh on both the leader and the person sitting across the table. You prepare for them. You think through your wording. You try to anticipate the questions or the reactions. You think about tone. You think about timing. Even when they're necessary and approached with care, those conversations often leave a lingering sense of uncertainty. The leader may walk away thinking, "Glad that's done," while the person on the receiving end walks away wondering what it really meant to their future in the building. You may resolve the issue, but the relationship can feel unsettled.

Leaders often underestimate how long that unsettled feeling lasts. It's not the content that lingers, it's the insecurity. It's the wondering.

It's the space between what the leader intended and how the person experienced the interaction. Leaders can't avoid tough conversations, but we can choose what comes next, and what comes next matters just as much as the conversation itself.

> Leaders can't avoid tough conversations, but we can choose what comes next, and what comes next matters just as much as the conversation itself.

Correction without connection feels like judgment. Connection afterward doesn't erase the awkwardness, but it keeps the relationship from getting stuck there. What people need most after a hard moment isn't perfection, and it isn't a grand gesture. It's proof that the relationship still has room to breathe. They need a sign that the moment was a moment and not a verdict.

Mr. Bright didn't need a formal structure or a flowchart. He simply understood that when a relationship dips, the leader must take the first step toward rebuilding it. Not because the person "deserves" it or because the issue wasn't real, but because people need to know that one tough moment doesn't define them. In many cases, the follow-up matters more than the correction. It shows people that they still belong, that the relationship is intact, and that the leader sees them as more than that moment.

Rebuilding connection after a difficult interaction isn't about sugarcoating accountability or avoiding direct conversations. It's about reinforcing trust in the aftermath. When leaders take the initiative to reconnect, it signals that accountability and belonging can coexist. It reminds the person that they are valued beyond the mistake or the moment of correction. It keeps the relationship moving instead of freezing it in the shadow of one uncomfortable interaction.

After a difficult interaction, leaders have an opportunity to step back into the person's space in a way that communicates stability,

BUILD BACK RELATIONSHIPS

respect, and care. It might be a check-in, a genuine question about how things are going, or simply being present and approachable in the days that follow. These small moments remind people that the tough conversation is *part* of the relationship, not the *whole* relationship.

I truly believe that when something cracks a relationship, the leader often has the best opportunity to repair it. People often wait to see if the leader's behavior toward them changes. They want to know if the conversation shifted the leader's view of them. They watch for clues, a greeting, a question, a simple hello. The smallest signals carry the biggest weight in the days that follow.

Mr. Bright modeled that long before I understood it, and it continues to shape how I think about leadership today. You can address the issue and still build the person. You can hold the line and still hold the relationship. Often the most important work you do comes after the hard conversation, when you step back into the person's world and show them they still belong.

This is where the practices of recognizing, acknowledging, and extending come alive. Recognition starts with noticing that the relationship dipped. Acknowledgment is naming effort, growth, or humanity in a way that reinforces identity. Extension is making sure the story doesn't stop there, it's carrying the connection forward, letting it move to another moment, another interaction, another space where belonging can take root again. None of this needs to be dramatic. None of it needs to be formal, but it needs to be intentional. People gravitate toward leaders who treat tough conversations as part of growth, not the end of trust.

Great leaders don't rebuild relationships with complexity. They rebuild them with consistency. They take the first step. They refuse to let one moment stand as the whole story. They show up often enough that trust has a rhythm again. The moment leaders begin leading that way, something shifts in the entire environment. People breathe differently. They trust differently. They show up differently because the moment you begin seeing people beyond their hardest moments, they begin seeing themselves beyond those moments, too.

> Great leaders don't rebuild relationships with complexity. They rebuild them with consistency.

The question that carries you out of this chapter is the same question that guided Mr. Bright all those years ago: Who needs you to take the first step toward rebuilding, and what's stopping you from getting there?

Core Value Connection

Manageable
Tomorrow, take one small step toward repairing a relationship—acknowledge a misstep, reopen a conversation, or simply show up with humility. Repair begins with presence, not perfection.

Meaningful
Think about a relationship that feels strained. Reflect on the part of the tension that is within your control to address and what a first step might look like.

Magnetic
If rebuilding relationships became a cultural norm here, how would conflict—and recovery from it—look different?

CHAPTER 12

Every Interaction Matters

The smallest moments create the longest memories

"A single act of kindness throws out roots in all directions."
—Amelia Earhart

If you've ever spent time in an elementary school lunchroom, you know it's the kind of organized chaos that is not easily described. Kids come in on a thirty-minute rotation, somehow manage to get their food, find a seat, eat half of it, trade the other half, and still have enough time left to create a level of noise that makes you question whether human ears were designed for this kind of environment. It's loud, it's messy, it's joyful, and a great place to watch kids be themselves.

One day I was in the back of the lunchroom talking with another principal when the first graders started rolling in, dancing, skipping, sliding, loud, happy, totally unfiltered. I didn't want to smile too much because I knew we had to keep some order in the room, and safety for everyone there, and all the things that crept into my head, but the smile was definitely visible. As I'm standing there, a little boy named Otto wraps himself around my leg like he's trying to keep me from boarding a flight. I look down and say, "Hey buddy, how's it going?" And he looks up at me with this expression like I had just personally ruined his entire week. "How come you're not so excited to see me?" he said. I kind of laughed and told him I was excited, and he shot back, "Well, you didn't say it!" and took off running to his table.

I stood there confused for a second before it clicked. Every morning when I greeted kids at the front door, I always started with the same line: "I am so excited to see you!" And every time I said it, Otto lit up. He expected it. It became part of the way he experienced me. But here in the lunchroom, I wasn't really with him. I was in the room, sure, but I wasn't fully present. He felt the difference immediately. In his six-year-old brain, something didn't match, and he named it.

That moment reminded me that every interaction speaks to who you are. Every single interaction. Not just the ones you prepare for, not just the ones you nail, not just the ones that happen in front of an audience. All of them. They all stack up. They build or they subtract. There are no neutral moments. That stacking effect is rhythm. It's how people come to know you—not through a single interaction, but through the consistency of how you show up over time. And here's the part we don't get to control: We don't get to choose what people remember. Those moments don't just stand alone—they repeat, and repetition is how rhythm is formed.

> We don't get to choose what people remember.

People experience leadership not as a single interaction, but as a pattern they come to expect. What stood out to me in the lunchroom wasn't what stood out to Otto at all. He didn't care about the conversation I was having with the principal. He cared that the version of me he saw at the front door didn't show up for him in the cafeteria.

That's the truth about leadership. Who you are is how you lead, and who you are gets communicated in a thousand tiny moments long before anyone asks you to run a meeting or make a decision. It's like a Monet painting: up close it looks messy and blurry and chaotic, but when you pull back far enough you see the picture clearly. Your leadership identity is painted by every interaction over time. People don't judge you by the moment you think is important. They judge you by the moment that mattered to them.

A few years after the Otto moment, I had another reminder, one that came six years after I thought the interaction ended. I was walking down the hallway one morning when a fifth grader yelled out, "Sanfelippo! What's the joke of the day?" I froze. I had no idea what he was talking about. I told him I'd think of one and circle back. I walked away confused…until it hit me halfway through the day. When he was in kindergarten, six years earlier, I used to walk around in the mornings and tell the joke of the day. And when I say "joke," I mean the kind of ridiculous material that makes even dad jokes sound edgy. I only did it for a couple of weeks, but apparently, in that short window, it became a memory that stuck.

So I walked into his classroom that afternoon and told the joke: "Don't trust stairs…they're always up to something." The kid looked at me like he'd been waiting years for this moment. "It's the joke of the day!" he yelled. And then the whole class joined him because they all remembered, too. Something I barely remembered doing had carved out a place in their story.

That's the second lesson: when we start something without intention and stop it without explanation, people will assume it wasn't that important to us. Which is confusing, because it mattered to them. They don't get to see your internal reasoning, your schedule, your stress, your to-do list. They only see the interaction. And when that interaction disappears without warning, it leaves a mark, sometimes small, sometimes big, but always a mark.

What these stories taught me is that, as leaders, it is both easier *and* harder to control the narrative than it used to be. Easier because the tools allow us to tell stories in a way that is accurate. Harder, because now everyone can tell a story from a device that they carry on them at all times and has an instant connection to thousands, perhaps millions, of people on the other side. We used to tell staff members, "When you talk to kids or parents, pretend that what you say will end up on the front page of the newspaper tomorrow." That was our way of reminding them to be intentional with their words and actions. The front page has changed now. It's not twenty-four hours away, it's five seconds away. It's a video. It's a screenshot. It's a post. We don't even get a chance to gather ourselves before the moment is shared. Leadership doesn't get the buffer it once had.

This chapter isn't about avoiding getting caught in a bad moment. It's about owning the truth that every interaction is a chance to narrate your own story. That choice gets made every interaction at a time.

You don't have to be perfect. You have to be aware. You have to be present enough to realize that the way you greet someone in the hallway becomes part of the picture they paint of you. The way you listen in a meeting becomes part of the picture. The way you respond when you're frustrated, or tired, or surprised, or overwhelmed, those become part of the picture, too. Presence isn't about perfection. It's about consistency. It's about the rhythm people come to expect when they experience you again and again. When people see you, they're not only seeing the moment, but they're also seeing the collection of moments that came before it.

This is why Personal Rhythm matters so deeply and why it is first. Chapters 1–6 are the foundation. Self-awareness steadies you. Intentional energy directs you. Joy keeps you grounded. Seeing greatness helps you notice what matters. All of that shows up in the way you walk into a room. Every interaction before the meeting shapes the meeting.

Your presence walks into a room ahead of your words. If your body language is tense, people brace. If you walk in rushed, people quiet down. If you walk in grounded and human, people exhale. Your role will always arrive before your personality unless your relationships get there first.

Every interaction matters because every interaction is an opportunity to connect, to build trust, to repair trust, to extend belief, to remind people who you are, and to

> **Your role will always arrive before your personality unless your relationships get there first.**

give yourself a better chance tomorrow than you had today. The interactions stack. They build the picture. They shape the perception. And in a world where every moment can be captured, shared, repeated, and replayed, awareness isn't optional. It's part of the job.

Awareness alone isn't enough. This is also the point where small, intentional behaviors make a massive difference. Tiny resets that take ten seconds. Something as simple as taking one deep breath before you turn the corner into a busy hallway. Pausing with your hand on the doorframe to remind yourself, "Bring the best version of you." Sending a quick text to someone who fills your tank, a colleague or a friend, right before you step into a tough meeting, not to get a response but to shift your mindset. Some people tap a spot on the wall they pass every day, the way athletes hit a tunnel sign before taking the field. Some people have a phrase they whisper under their breath, something grounding like, "Walk with purpose," or "Be present," or "Lead with calm." These aren't grand strategies. They're small anchors that help you reset who you are before people experience you. And the more consistently you do them, the more naturally you walk into the next moment as the person you want to be. I could list pages and pages of suggestions on how to ground yourself, but when it comes down to it, the only thing that matters is that whatever you do matters to you. Sending a text is my thing. Putting my phone in my back pocket when I walk into a conversation so my hands are free and I am not distracted in the conversation is my thing. Moving my body in a hallway conversation so there are not people moving over the shoulder of the person I am talking to is my thing. All of them give me the best chance. None of them may give you the best chance, and that's why this work is so personal. Know yourself well enough to know what is going to give you the best chance and start there. With one thing..then build.

> **Every interaction matters because every interaction could be the one they talk about for the rest of their lives.**

We don't have to love the responsibility of every interaction, but we do have to acknowledge that it's real. Every interaction matters because every interaction could be the one they talk about for the rest of their lives. The more intentional you become about the moments you create, the more influence you have in the moments that matter most.

Core Value Connection

Manageable
Tomorrow, choose one interaction and treat it as if it might be the one a person remembers for the rest of their life. Small interactions can carry unexpected weight.

Meaningful
Think about an interaction someone had with you that stayed with you. Reflect on why it lasted and what it revealed about the power of seemingly ordinary moments.

Magnetic
If every interaction shaped the legacy of our culture, what would I want those moments to collectively say?

CHAPTER 13

In the Absence of Knowledge

You are either the narrator of your story or
the character in someone else's

"If you don't share your truth, someone else will write it for you."
—Brené Brown

When I took the superintendent job in Fall Creek, Wisconsin, I walked into a district that had seen five superintendents in six years. You don't need a leadership degree to understand what that means. People were tired. People were wary. People had seen leaders arrive with plans and leave before those plans ever mattered. While I believed I could lead a group of people, a question kept creeping into my head: *Would the environment even allow me the opportunity to start?* Even though I could not control what happened before I came, the thought of the impact it had made me question if I could get it started. Even the mindset of asking myself *if they would allow me the opportunity to start* was an excuse I was making before I even started. A way to get myself out. A crutch. An exit. Before I even started. Would it have been easier to know that I would stay for twelve years and that the school district and community would be the best professional thing that ever happened to me? Sure…but we don't have that luxury.

Getting the fear of failure out of my own head was the first step. I knew if we could get a few early wins, small but meaningful ones, it would create some momentum, and the momentum would carry us into the next phase. I also knew that if I wasn't careful, I could easily become another chapter in a long book of turnover. Thinking about what the building could look like in ten years was futile. I started thinking about what it could look like in ten days.

The challenge, of course, is that you don't know what you're walking into until you walk into it. You're trusting that everyone is being honest about the culture, the dynamics, the history, the parts no one says out loud. You're trusting that the story they're telling you matches the one you'll actually live. And even with all that information, you still have to rely on who you are, your identity, your values, your presence, because those are the things that will determine whether you can help a group move forward.

Very early in my first year, the emphasis had to be on making the uncomfortable, comfortable. If the only time they saw the boss was when something was wrong or needed, that was the expectation every time I walked into the room. The presence was intentional and purposeful as we tried to build momentum. If you show up consistently enough, people eventually stop bracing when you walk in the door. One day I walked into a four-year-old kindergarten classroom. As soon as I stepped inside, one of the students ran up, pointed at my head, and yelled, "What's your name? Where's your hair?" The teacher smiled and shrugged as if to say, "Two very relevant questions." I got down to his level to introduce myself, and halfway through my second sentence, he bolted. Just took off. No warning. Just ran away and went back to playing with cars.

IN THE ABSENCE OF KNOWLEDGE

He had no idea what I did. He also represented the thoughts of everyone in that community. I had just become a character in the story. I wasn't the narrator of my story, so I couldn't possibly be the narrator of their story yet. They were still responding to whatever story they'd lived through with the leaders who came before me. That may or may not explain why there were five superintendents in six years, but it sure didn't help. The truth is that in the absence of knowledge, people tend to make up their own.

Tom Murray, ASCD best-selling author and Director of Innovation at Future Ready Schools references what many refer to as the "Curse of Knowledge," the moment when leaders become so familiar with their work, their systems, and their expectations that they forget what it felt like not to know them. It's not arrogance; it's proximity. When something is clear in our own heads, we assume it must be clear to everyone else. And that assumption quietly erodes trust.

The danger is that familiarity starts masquerading as clarity. Leaders say things like, "We already talked about this," or "It's in the email," or "They should know by now." But communication isn't about what's said; it's about what's understood. When leaders tap out the rhythm of the song in their own head, they forget that others can't hear the melody. To them, it's just noise.

Murray's work pushes leaders to slow down and make the implicit explicit. To break things into smaller steps. To say the important things again, not because people aren't capable, but because clarity creates confidence. He reminds us that repetition isn't redundancy when the message matters; it's reassurance.

Tom also names something leaders rarely see while it's happening: invisible distance. It shows up when clarity exists in your head but never quite makes it into the room. You're already standing on the other side of the bridge, wondering why people aren't moving, without realizing they can't see the bridge yet. When that gap exists, people don't disengage immediately. They hesitate. They second-guess themselves. They stop asking questions because they don't want to look behind. Over time, confusion quietly turns into compliance, and compliance never builds great cultures. Intentional leaders slow down just enough to bring others with them, sharing not just the decision, but the thinking behind it. What feels repetitive to a leader often feels reassuring to a team. When leaders are grounded in who they are, they're more willing to slow down long enough to make sure others can follow. And that awareness changes everything.

This is especially critical in moments of transition, uncertainty, or change. When leaders assume understanding instead of building it, people fill in the gaps with whatever story they already know. But when leaders communicate with empathy, patience, and intention, they remove guesswork. And when guesswork disappears, people stop bracing and start engaging.

Clarity doesn't water leadership down. It strengthens it. Because people don't lose trust when leaders repeat themselves, they lose trust when leaders assume. When leaders close those gaps with intention instead of assumption, they give people fewer reasons to brace and more reasons to trust.

What they make up is almost always based on their experience leading up to that point. Ironically, when you are going into a new organization, the experience is not with you, it's with the person who held that job title before you. The interesting thing is that their experience, specifically in a school, happens in a pretty spread-out timeline. The staff had an experience the previous year. The students had an experience the previous year that may not have even included an interaction with the leader in the school. The community goes back to the experience they had in schools. Which, for some, could have been decades ago. All those experiences come to the forefront when new leadership is established. And all those experiences, though we had nothing to do with them, need to be validated. We build from where people are, not where we hoped they were. Expecting them to be at a certain place just because you know it is going to get better is, at the least irresponsible, and could be egotistical.

If you're a leader in any organization, the people walking into your building are comparing you to the last experience they had, whether it was five months ago or five years ago. If they've only been there once and it went poorly, that's what they're carrying with them. If they've been there dozens of times, all those experiences stack, and they shape the lens they walk in with.

The moment an adult walks into an elementary building, they are transported right back to the age when they had their own school experience. The extra chicken sandwich they didn't get at lunch. The grade they thought was unfair. The teacher who loved them. The coach who didn't play them. Even if they haven't stepped into a school for twenty years, the feelings from twenty years ago walk through the door with them.

That's why identity matters so deeply in leadership. Who you are precedes what you do, but that has a tendency to get lost on the group you lead because of the person you succeeded. What they experience in you needs to be grounded in presence, clarity, and consistency. Alone they are important and essential to communication. Together, they help bridge the gap between communication and connection.

Presence comes from showing up before you need something and being human while you're there. Clarity comes from removing guesswork and giving people enough detail that they don't have to fill in the blanks on their own. And consistency comes from doing it day after day, long before the big decisions or the hard moments show up. All of them create connections that are talked about vs communication that is only sometimes remembered. It also helps with ownership vs. compliance.

> Presence comes from showing up before you need something and being human while you're there.

Here's an example of how this plays out in real time. If I call a parent and say, "Your son is great," they'll smile, maybe thank me, and move on with their day. It may or may not come up in conversation with the student the next time a parent sees him. It may be the discussion at the dinner table or on a ride to baseball practice that night. But if I call and say, "Hi Andrea, I was in a third-grade classroom this morning and your sophomore son Aidan was sitting on the carpet reading to a little girl. She looked up at him like he was a superhero. He answered every one of her questions, and you could see in her face how safe and special she felt. I just want to say thank you, because my guess is he learned that at home," then something different happens. I've now given her a time, a place, a scene, a sense of what it felt like to watch it. I put her in the classroom. I let her feel the moment. That story has a better chance to be told at the dinner table. That story, more often than not, also gets told to someone else outside of the immediate family. A grandparent, a neighbor, at a book group, at work the next day…all of those are opportunities to build momentum. When we help people connect to the emotion of the event there is a better chance for the event to be talked about long after the event takes place.

I also did something else without saying it directly, I told her where I was. "I was in the classroom and this is what I saw." It gives more context to the story and places you right in the middle of it. You didn't hear about it from someone, you were there. "I was in the hallway and this is what I saw." "I was at the game and this is what I saw." You shouldn't have to tell people where you are, but when they don't know, this kind of clarity helps build trust. It fills in the gaps so they don't fill them with whatever story they've been holding for twenty years.

Identity isn't built through announcements or newsletters. It's built through the way you narrate your work with presence, clarity, and consistency. It's built through the little interactions before the big ones. It's built through the rhythm you bring into a space long before you ever lead a meeting in that space.

IN THE ABSENCE OF KNOWLEDGE

And here's the hard part, you don't get to choose what people remember. You don't get to decide which moment becomes the defining interaction. You don't get to control which story sticks. People remember what matters to *them*, not what you hoped they'd remember. They remember it based on how they felt in the moment.

That can feel overwhelming, but it's actually an invitation, and a powerful one. When you understand that every interaction contributes to the painting people are creating of you, it shifts how you show up. Every conversation, every hallway exchange, every email, every pause before responding, every expression on your face, it's all part of the portrait people carry of you. Those interactions don't need to be perfect, but they need to be intentional. The more intentional you are about each one, the more influence you have when it matters most.

When I started in Fall Creek, I didn't know if I'd get six months, a year, or two years. I just knew that if I stayed true to who I was, and stayed consistent in how I showed up, I would give myself the best possible chance to lead the group. What surprised me most wasn't how people responded to me, but how they responded to each other. There were incredible things happening every single day in that district, but even the people in the building didn't always see it. Once they did and saw greatness in someone else, they recognized their own reflection in it and started talking about it. They started sharing it. They started believing in it.

Momentum doesn't start with a program. It starts with identity. Again, identity grows through presence, clarity, and consistency, especially in the moments when people don't have enough information and fill in the blanks with whatever story they know best.

You may not have been the author of the first chapter people bring into the room with them, but you absolutely get to shape the chapters that come next, and when you lead from who you are, you give people a reason to keep reading.

Core Value Connection

Manageable
Tomorrow, proactively share one brief piece of information with someone who needs it before they have to ask. Removing uncertainty strengthens trust.

Meaningful
Recall a moment when lack of information created frustration or misunderstanding. Reflect on what small communication shift would have prevented it.

Magnetic
If transparency became our default process, how would communication—and trust—shift across the organization?

CHAPTER 14

The 30-Second Legacy

How brief moments leave lasting impressions
*"In the end, it's not the years in your life that count,
but the life in your years."*
—Abraham Lincoln

After a speaking event a few years ago, someone came up to me and asked, "Has this whole public speaking thing always come naturally to you?" I didn't even hesitate. I said, "No. Not even close." They looked surprised, probably because they had just watched me on a stage having the time of my life. That's not how it started. I told a piece of the following story in *Lead From Where You Are*, but feel like the deeper dive fits perfectly here:

The truth is the first time I remember speaking in front of a group of people was in seventh grade, and it went about as poorly as it could go. So when my eighth-grade English teacher told us we'd be memorizing and reciting a poem in front of the entire class, you can imagine how thrilled I was about that activity. We were supposed to research a list of poems, choose one, and submit it ahead of time. I think we've established that I was not exactly the most academically enthusiastic student of all time, so I absolutely did not do that. When he got to my name, I was clearly not paying attention because I looked up at the board and picked the first poem I saw: *The Midnight Ride of Paul Revere*. You would've thought I had announced that I was dropping out of school. Heads snapped around. A couple kids laughed. My best friend was sitting next to me and I remember him saying, louder than he probably intended, "Ohhhh noooo…"

What I didn't realize, what truly every other person in the room already knew, is that it was the longest poem on the list. Had I even taken three seconds to look at the poems, I would have known to pick one that was six lines. Instead, I chose the one that lasted roughly the length of a short film. The bigger problem was that now I was committed, because everyone had heard me say it out loud. What happened next was not out of engagement or desire to get a good grade, it was out of sheer terror and the knowledge that if I screwed it up, the whole class was going to know.

So I worked. Hard. Harder than I had worked on almost anything at that point. And when the day came, I stood up, heart pounding, palms sweating, and I recited the entire thing. From memory. Word for word. I'm certain that I didn't nail the pacing and probably sounded like I was selling something at auction, but I remember the feeling when I finished. I took this giant breath, half relief, half disbelief, and asked if there were any questions.

One girl, two rows back and two desks to the right, raised her hand. Her tone was gentle, almost warm. And she said, "I'm really proud of you."

That's it. Five words. I remember the way she said it. I remember the look on her face. I remember the confidence it gave me, this rush of pride that had nothing to do with the poem and everything to do with being seen. I didn't become a better speaker in that moment, but I became a braver one, and I wanted to do it again. Not read the poem, but get the feeling. I know I wasn't a great student, but as I reflect on that day, I must have been an awful student. Because the story about my speech didn't end in the classroom. Other kids heard about it, and teachers stopped me in the hallway or said something in their class later that day. Knowing what I know now, it was probably a conversation in the staff lounge at lunch that started with, "You guys are not going to believe this…"

I still think about that moment, because it taught me something I didn't have the language for back then: It's not the time…it's what you do with the time…every time. A ninety-second poem became a catalyst because of four seconds of kindness. It wasn't the speech that mattered. It was the sentence. Sometimes I feel like I'm always chasing that feeling, recognizing the impact, and making sure people feel seen the way I felt…and that was almost forty years ago.

> It's not the time…it's what you do with the time…every time.

That's the heart of the 30-second legacy. It's not about squeezing more in. It's about being more intentional with the time you already have. If I asked someone to stand on one leg with their eyes closed for thirty seconds or stand nose-to-nose with a stranger for thirty seconds (which I will do EVERY time I speak to a group), it would feel like an eternity. But if I asked that same person to send a positive text message to someone who has had an impact on their life, those same thirty seconds would go so fast and that intentional use of time could spark a feeling in another person which could lead to a better day for them, or getting a text message back from that person makes it a better day for you. Manageable (how many texts do you think you send in a day?), Meaningful (the more real the text is, the more meaningful it is to the participant…the whole "Your son is great" vs "I was in a classroom and this is what I saw"), and it's Magnetic (you get a text back, they send a text to someone else…everyone wins).

Working in organizations can become monotonous. We build big plans that take months or years to see through, and half the time we don't even know if the plan "worked" because so many factors are affecting the outcome. People get tired waiting for wins. They lose momentum. They lose hope. That's why I kept coming back to this idea: big change isn't sustained by big moments; it's sustained by little ones. The Recognize → Acknowledge → Extend mindset is not a task list; it's a way of noticing the world. When people start noticing the good in each other, they create small wins that stack into something meaningful. The 30-second legacy is the fuel behind that mindset. It's the reminder that *every small act, every encouraging word, every moment of recognition buys someone one more step forward*–and sometimes that's all they needed.

The practical part is simple; name effort when you see it. Not the result. Not the product. Not the performance. The effort. The try. The courage. Five words in an 8th grade classroom changed things for me. I walked with more confidence in the building, but I am still referencing it as an anchor I go back to decades later. Five words could change something for someone at any and every age. That, in and of itself, should be enough motivation to do it for others. We never grow out of needing to be seen.

> **We never grow out of needing to be seen.**

The smallest moments push people forward, but they also teach people what leadership looks like, even when you're not trying to teach anything at all.

We used to award "Principal of the Day" to one student in our school. It was one of my favorite traditions. The student would spend the day shadowing me, walking hallways, visiting classrooms, supervising recess, doing announcements, sitting in on meetings. (They did not answer emails, which I still think would have been hilarious.) We'd end the day with a picture, a certificate, some school gear, and a snack bag. They thought they were getting a big deal; truth is, I may have gotten more out of it than they did.

One year, a kindergarten student named Jake was selected. The day before, I called his parents, walked him through what the day would look like, and rearranged my schedule so he'd get the full range of experiences without having to sit quietly through 165 emails. When he arrived the next morning, he was dressed professionally, or at least professionally for a six-year-old, which meant a button-down shirt and dress pants. He was ready.

We started by meeting with the secretary, then walked into my office to do the morning announcements. When morning classes settled, we began our walk around the school. Our first stop was his kindergarten room. Without a script, he walked right in, shook the teacher's hand, and said, "My name is Jake, and I'm the principal today. So if you need anything, please let me know."

His teacher melted on the spot. I smiled. He kept going through the room like he'd been doing the job for years. We visited more classrooms, greeted students, checked in on recess, and then headed to the cafeteria for lunch duty. He was a natural. He may have asked every adult in the building how they were doing and if they needed anything. He had a presence…did I mention he was six? There was a moment in the cafeteria when I thought, "I might be out of a job."

At some point during our walk, I did something I always tried to do. I bent down, picked up a wrapper on the floor, and tossed it in the trash. I didn't make a speech about it. I didn't point to a sign. I just did it because it needed to be done. We finished the day, took the pictures of him at the principal's desk and meeting with the secretary, doing the announcements, and sent everything home.

A few weeks later, I got an email from his dad. They had been walking together down the hallway toward a game, and Jake kept bending down to pick up wrappers. His dad asked him, "Buddy, what are you doing?" And Jake said, "This is what we do here."

Something that leaders know, but often fail to keep in mind is that *people are always learning from you, even when you're not teaching.*

You don't get to choose what they notice. You don't get to choose what they repeat. You don't get to choose which thirty seconds become their definition of "how we do things here." What we model is what we get. So the question becomes: What are we doing to make sure that what we model is actually what we want repeated?

> **What are we doing to make sure that what we model is actually what we want repeated?**

That moment with Jake is the whole chapter in one scene. He didn't say it because I told him to. He said it because he saw it. Leadership grows in the small, unplanned, unnoticed behaviors we carry between the big moments. It grows in the seconds when we think no one is paying attention. Kids learn that way. Adults do, too. Side note: I recently got a text from Jake's dad with an audio recording of a voicemail we left when Jake was the Principal of the Day as a kindergartner—fifteen years ago. Jake is now twenty-one and has started his own business. Shocker, right?

The connection between the two stories, the eighth-grade girl who changed my outlook with one sentence and the kindergarten student who modeled leadership with one gesture shows us that legacy lives in the small moments. Not the meetings. Not the memos. Not the announcements. The moments. The thirty seconds when someone is watching, listening, wondering, and deciding who you are.

The part that makes me smile the most is that these moments are always available. You don't need a title. You don't need a position. You don't need a formal plan. You don't need a big stage. You need to be present enough to honor the next thirty seconds. That's the opportunity. It doesn't mean you are going to get everything right all the time. What it does mean is that you walk into every interaction with more purpose and a better chance for people to walk out feeling valued.

There's a quiet power in choosing to see those moments. A sense of purpose. When we stop chasing the huge outcomes and start noticing the tiny openings, we realize how much influence we've had all along. Legacy isn't built by accident. It's built by awareness. By paying attention. By noticing what other people need in the moment and adjusting ourselves to meet them there.

That's the *direction* piece, even if we never say the word. When we treat the next thirty seconds like they matter, we point other people toward a version of themselves they didn't think they could reach. When we stay present instead of rushed, connected instead of distracted, intentional instead of accidental, we give ourselves—and those we serve—a better chance at the next moment. It's that simple and that hard.

Which brings me back to the poem.

I think about that day in eighth grade more often than anyone would expect. I think about twelve-year-old me, standing in front of my class, terrified and sweating through polyester. I think about the girl who raised her hand and said, "I'm really proud of you." I think about the surge of pride that made me want to do it again, the feeling that would years later become the reason I love speaking today. The reason I chase smiles and laughter and those quiet head nods when someone realizes they're capable of more than they thought.

That's the 30-second legacy.

Not the poem. Not the speech. Not the performance. The feeling. The kindness. The connection. The direction forward. We don't choose what people remember, but we *do* choose who we are in each moment.

Core Value Connection

Manageable
Tomorrow, take thirty seconds to make someone's day lighter—through a comment, a gesture, a check-in, or a brief acknowledgement. Short moments can create long memories.

Meaningful
Think about how quickly your mood can shift in thirty seconds. Reflect on what that reveals about the influence you have in everyday interactions.

Magnetic
If our school became known for the way we lift others in brief moments, how would that impact belonging?

Summary: The People Rhythm

The Personal Rhythm was about understanding who you are when you walk into the day; The People Rhythm is about understanding what happens the moment you walk into a room. These chapters live in the space between identity and influence, where leadership starts becoming something others can actually feel. You can know yourself, steady yourself, ground yourself, and still lose the moment the second you step into someone else's world if you don't understand the rhythm of people. The People Rhythm is what shapes how people experience you. It's how trust is built. It's how connection forms. It's how culture grows and how it breaks. Leadership is carried forward by people long before it is ever carried forward by strategy, and the People Rhythm is where that becomes real.

What becomes clear right away is that people don't respond to your position nearly as much as they respond to your presence. Anyone can walk into a room with a title, that title may actually get you into rooms, but you walk differently when you walk in with presence. If you rely on that title, the best that you can hope for from the group you lead is compliance. No one goes beyond their job title for someone who is so dependent on theirs. Presence is

> No one goes beyond their job title for someone who is so dependent on theirs.

what signals whether someone feels safe around you, whether they feel understood, or whether they need to brace themselves. The story about the moment in the kitchen when my presence was misinterpreted wasn't about behavior; it was about how people fill in the gaps with whatever experience they've had with you before that moment. It's a reminder that your presence arrives before your words do, and it carries the weight of every interaction you've had with that person up to that point. That weight is either grounding or anxiety-producing, depending on the rhythm you've created.

This rhythm shows up in powerful ways when leaders begin to realize how differently "checking in with" people feels compared to "checking up on" them. The difference between those two phrases seems small on the surface, but emotionally they live on opposite ends of the leadership spectrum. Checking up on people introduces tension, even when your intent is good. It carries with it the possibility of judgment, and whether you mean to or not, your presence becomes tied to pressure. But checking in with people changes everything. It makes your presence feel like support, like partnership, like someone who wants to walk with them instead of evaluate them. Ironically, the more you check in early, the less you ever have to check up on later. It doesn't eliminate having to check up on people, because again, people drift, but it does reduce the number of times you have to and even when you do, it feels different. When people experience your presence consistently, they feel steady when you arrive, not startled.

You can feel the impact of this the moment you enter a space where people are used to seeing you as an advocate for the work they do. They talk differently and share more openly. They let you into their world instead of guarding themselves from it. You can feel when the culture has shifted to checking in instead of checking up on, because trust becomes something lived rather than discussed. When people no longer waste emotional energy worrying about why you're there, they can use that energy on the work itself. This is one of the clearest signs

SUMMARY: THE PEOPLE RHYTHM

of a healthy People Rhythm: Your presence brings calm, not concern.

The Candy Hearts example is one of those tiny moments that reveals just how sensitive people are to the signals leaders send, especially the small ones. A sentence fragment. A glance. A nod. A shift in tone. Leaders sometimes imagine that the big conversations carry the most weight, but the longer you lead, the more you know it's the little, seemingly forgettable interactions at the time that end up shaping the strongest memories. People remember how you made them feel before they remember anything you said. The smallest signals shape how people interpret your leadership far more than any staff meeting ever will.

That's also why consistency matters so much. People will tell you their favorite leaders are charismatic or inspiring, but when you dig deeper, you almost always find something different underneath: reliability. The people considered "everyone's favorite" are almost never everyone's favorite because of the big moments; they are everyone's favorite because of who they are in the small moments. They are steady. They listen. They show up. They don't make people guess which version of them is walking into the room, even when the job is hard or the day is chaotic or the circumstances are less than ideal, they are consistent.

That consistency gets tested the most in moments that don't feel smooth. Mr. Bright chose not to let a negative moment define our relationship. He didn't correct me once and move on. He rebuilt the relationship through presence, interaction, and intentional connection. The part that stuck with me was not the correction; it was the follow-up. It was the way he refused to let one moment become the whole story. Leaders often underestimate this part. We assume a difficult conversation begins and ends with the actual conversation, but the truth is that the real work happens afterward. Correction without connection feels like judgment. Correction followed by connection becomes trust.

This pattern repeats itself in schools, in healthcare, in private industry, and everywhere people work with people. A tough moment can either shrink the relationship or strengthen it, and leaders get to decide which direction it moves. When you go back into a person's space after a difficult interaction, with genuine humanity, you signal that they are more important than the moment. You remind them the relationship still has room to grow and show them they still belong. This is the heartbeat of the People Rhythm: reinforcing connection not only before and during meaningful moments, but after them as well.

The chapters that live in the middle of the People Rhythm speak to this in different ways. They highlight how every interaction matters, not because every interaction is dramatic, but because every interaction is cumulative. The quick hallway hello. The comment you didn't intend to sound sharp. The encouraging word that landed at the perfect time. The moment you paused instead of rushing past. Each of these things stacks on top of the others until people begin to form a storyline about who you are. That storyline becomes their expectation of you. I truly believe that most defining leadership moments take less than thirty seconds, and often you don't even realize the moment mattered until years later. The person you influenced remembers it vividly, the tone, the timing, the expression, while you move on thinking it was just an ordinary day.

This becomes even more complicated when silence gets involved, and how people fill in the blanks when they can't see what's happening behind the scenes. Leaders know they are having the tough conversations. They know the accountability work is happening. They know the follow-through is there. But because so much of leadership work must be done privately, people rarely see the full picture. When those gaps are left open long enough, the stories people imagine begin to feel real. It isn't usually malicious, people just try to make sense of their environment. They connect dots that don't belong together. They assume silence is indifference or avoidance instead of simply confidentiality or timing.

What protects leaders in those moments isn't visibility into the private work, it's the track record of presence before the moment ever

SUMMARY: THE PEOPLE RHYTHM

arrives. When people know your character, they trust your silence. When people have felt your consistency, your empathy, and your follow-through, they interpret the gaps with generosity instead of suspicion. This is the part leaders don't talk about enough. Presence isn't just a strategy for when things go well, it is your insurance policy for when things go sideways. It's what helps keep a tough moment from turning into a fractured relationship. It's what steadies people who don't have all the information. It doesn't ensure things will go the way you want or intended, but it helps, and gives you the best chance to lead through those moments where all the information is not, or cannot, be accessible to all.

> When people know your character, they trust your silence.

The People Rhythm also reveals that leaders who help build the strongest cultures are ones who create the strongest habits in the organization. They build a habit of noticing, being real, removing fear from the room, being steady when things around them are not, and making sure people aren't surprised by their presence. These habits become the emotional infrastructure of the building. I would love to tell you that 100% of the people in the building will feel like they belong, but I can't. What the People Rhythm does is give you the best chance to get the most people walking in every day with a sense of purpose because they know who they are matters to those around them.

What you see across all the chapters in the People Rhythm is a thread that keeps looping back to the same truth: people follow the leader before they follow the plan. They follow who you are, how you show up, and how you make them feel, not in one moment, but in the accumulation of many moments. They decide whether they trust you in those moments. They build their understanding of you through your timing. They form their perception of your leadership not just based on what you announce at a staff meeting, but based on how you navigate the hallway ten minutes later. This rhythm is more consistent, and honestly, more human.

As the People Rhythm closes, the shift becomes clear. Once you understand your presence, your pacing, your checking-in rhythm, your consistency, your follow-up, your communication, and the weight of every small interaction, you begin to see that leadership is not something you do occasionally, it's something you practice constantly. Influence is accumulated over time. Culture is not the product of large, dramatic moments. It's the result of steady, human ones that build on each other until trust becomes the default.

All this work leads to the Process Rhythm, where clarity, alignment, communication, and movement begin to take shape. It's where the direction of the organization becomes something everyone can feel, not just something written on a document. It's where leadership is more strategic, but it works substantially better when the Personal Rhythm and the People Rhythm are fully embedded. It is much harder to lead the process before you lead yourself and the people around you with consistency, presence, and trust. And that's where we're headed next.

PART III

The Process Rhythm

*Direction:
Moving People Forward*

CHAPTER 15

Model the Mission

People follow what they see, not what they hear

*"Example is not the main thing in influencing others.
It is the only thing."*
—Albert Schweitzer

Before leaders ever say a word, the mission is already being modeled. Every hallway interaction, every response to a mistake, every moment of clarity or confusion, people are watching. They're learning what matters, what doesn't, and what "good enough" looks like. And whether we want to admit it or not, organizations don't become what we announce, they become what we model. That modeling creates the Process Rhythm of an organization. It's the steady pattern people follow when deciding how much effort to give, how much ownership to take, and what "good work" actually looks like here.

I see it every time I speak to a group. I'll tell the audience, "Raise your hand as high as you can." Hundreds of hands go up. Then after two seconds, I say, "Great. Now raise it a little higher." Every single time, hands go higher. Laughs happen under their breath with the realization of what happened and I ask, "What's that all about?" The direction was crystal clear. But the effort? The effort matched the meaning they attached to it, which, in that moment, was basically zero. We're in an auditorium. They just met me. No stakes. No connection. No reason to give their best.

People fall back to their default, not because they're lazy or disengaged, but because we haven't given them the clarity, the meaning, or the connection that pulls them beyond average effort. This is where manageable, meaningful, magnetic ties in. Can they do it? Will it mean something to them? Will it connect to something they care about? When the answer is yes, effort goes up. When the answer is no, hands stay at shoulder height even when they could have reached the ceiling. And they didn't even know it.

People drift. It's one of the most reliable patterns in human behavior. Not because people are trying to do less, avoid responsibility, or check out, but because drift is what happens in the absence of clarity, connection, or meaning. When direction isn't clear, people settle. They stay competent but stop stretching. They complete tasks but stop owning the work. They show up, but they stop leaning in. Not out of apathy, but out of uncertainty.

Drift isn't a character flaw. *Drift is a leadership gap.* In the absence of a clear process rhythm, people default to whatever pace feels safest or easiest in the moment. That's not laziness—that's human nature.

You see it everywhere. Education. Healthcare. Retail. Manufacturing. Restaurants. The setting changes. The stakes change. The pattern doesn't. When leaders don't model what direction looks like, even strong, capable people slowly slide back toward average without realizing it. People don't drift because they don't care. They drift because no one helped them see where to aim, and how to keep moving once they started.

The same thing happens in schools, stores, restaurants, clinics, honestly, everywhere. Walk into a mechanic shop, a doctor's office, or a restaurant and within thirty seconds you can tell what kind of leadership exists there. Not because of posters or slogans or mission

MODEL THE MISSION

statements on the wall, but because people are modeling whatever has been modeled for them. That's why some places feel alive and others feel like everyone is running on fumes. Nobody wakes up saying, "I can't wait to give my most mediocre effort today." People drift toward minimal effort when meaning is missing and modeling is inconsistent.

> **People drift toward minimal effort when meaning is missing and modeling is inconsistent.**

That's why modeling matters and building capacity is the antidote to isolation. Leaders who model the mission don't create followers, they create leaders.

Our school was very lucky to be recognized on a national level as an Innovative School multiple times. With that, we were able to travel to conferences across the country and present our process to groups. If you've been to a conference you know that some presentations are dynamic and some are informative. The gold is when you find a balance between the two. Make people, laugh, smile, think, and feel and you have something that they will remember long after the presentation takes place. Putting a process together that would give people the best chance to remember our group was almost as important as the content we were going to share. The best content, not remembered, turns into "I think they said something about…" or "That was a great story, but it could never work here" kind of moment for the participants, so we wanted to make sure we gave everyone in that room the best chance, which included the group we had presenting. Before anyone presented publicly, we had them practice the process with a small group, including me. We kept preparation simple: story → connection → action. At this point, you should see that modeled throughout this entire book. I modeled what it looked like in staff meetings, our own professional development and when I spoke to groups outside the organization. We named the three parts out loud, and then they crafted their own. They would come back again and again to refine it, not because I demanded it, but because excellence had become the expectation we lived, not the quote we had attached to our email or a saying posted on a wall. That repetition is what turned expectations into a process rhythm—clear enough to guide people, flexible enough to let them lead.

When they did present, they walked the halls of those conferences like they owned the place. Confidence. Pride. When the school board later asked if the trip had been worth the time out of the classroom, one of our teachers looked at her team, then at the board, and said, "We felt like rockstars." That wasn't about ego. It was about identity. It was about seeing themselves as leaders because they had been supported by each other. If you want people to lead, you have to let them lead, even when they won't lead exactly the way you would. Actually, especially then. Giving them a blueprint to create their own narrative is empowering for the individual and still sets the tone for how we want others to walk away from experiences.

This is why modeling creates momentum. It offers parameters without prescribing personality. It's the whole point of Intention → Connection → Direction. You model what intention looks like. You connect with people so there is meaning with multiple people. Then you provide direction that leaves room for ownership. People don't do their best work because they were told to, they do their best work because they can see themselves in the work.

> People don't do their best work because they were told to, they do their best work because they can see themselves in the work.

This applies to mission statements and vision statements, too. The words may not mean anything to people who had no role in creating them. But behaviors? Behaviors connect everyone to the mission. Modeling isn't optional and it isn't for some people, it's for everyone.

The key is narrowing the non-negotiables. If everything is important, nothing is. I cared deeply about being present, always. I cared about listening to understand, not respond. I cared about the fact that every interaction matters. There were other things I didn't care as much about. Dress code? Not a hill I was going to die on. Someone needing to leave early because of an appointment? Go. Handle what you need to handle. Leaders burn out when they expect excellence in fifty areas instead of five. Staff burn out the same way.

So we strip away what doesn't matter. We model what does. We raise our hand higher because the work means more, and we give people a chance to lead, not by demanding perfection but by creating parameters that let them own the process.

When people know what excellence looks like, when they've seen you model how to give direction and how to receive it, when they feel permission to lead even if their version looks different from yours, *they stop waiting for you and they start leading with you.* This is the Process Rhythm in action. It's how leaders turn values into behaviors, behaviors into habits, and habits into a way of working people can trust and repeat. Modeling the mission doesn't make you the hero. It makes everyone around you capable of becoming one.

Core Value Connection

Manageable
Tomorrow, choose one routine action—a greeting, a meeting start, or a hallway moment—and intentionally model one core value through behavior rather than words. People learn the mission by watching it lived.

Meaningful
Write down two moments this week when your behavior aligned with your mission and two when it didn't. Reflect on what each moment reinforced for others.

Magnetic
If someone wrote our mission based only on what I modeled today, what would they write—and what do I want them to write instead?

CHAPTER 16

The Expert's Space

Great leaders don't walk into rooms to prove; they walk in to understand

"Leaders who don't listen will eventually be surrounded by people who have nothing to say."
—Andy Stanley

Recently, I landed at an airport and headed toward the shuttle that would take me to the rental car center. About halfway through the ride, a man across the aisle suddenly leaned forward and called out, "Hey, are you sure this is the right way?" The driver didn't flinch. Didn't turn around. Didn't defend himself. He just kept driving, because of course he knew the way. This was literally the route he drives all day, every day. And I sat there thinking, *My man...this is his whole job. Maybe trust him.* I didn't say it out loud, but I laughed to myself as I walked off the shuttle. And then the leadership question shows up, the one that always seems to pop into my head: How many times have I done the exact same thing as a leader? How many times have I walked into someone else's space and, without meaning to, questioned the person who knew that space best?

As I thought about it, I started replaying moments from my early years as a principal, moments when I walked into classrooms with the mindset that I had something to "fix" or "suggest" or "adjust," even though I wasn't the one in the room every day. I wasn't navigating twenty-five personalities, five learning needs, unexpected student dynamics, or the sudden curveballs that show up between 8:00 and 3:30. I hadn't designed the routines, built the relationships, or managed the energy in that space. But I would sometimes step in as if my snapshot of the moment carried more weight than the expertise of the person living the reality.

I never meant it that way, but intent doesn't erase impact. It doesn't matter that our hearts are in the right place if the moment lands differently for the person in front of us. A leader's question, when it stands alone, can feel like doubt. A comment without context can feel like criticism. And the less someone sees you, the more likely they are to interpret your question as judgment, not curiosity. Being a good teacher doesn't make you a good leader of good teachers when you forget how much work it takes to be a good teacher. Everyone is busy with their own responsibilities, including the leader, but when you forget what it takes to do the work

> Being a good teacher doesn't make you a good leader of good teachers when you forget how much work it takes to be a good teacher.

in that space, your leadership loses impact. That shuttle ride reminded me that leadership isn't just about what we say when we enter a space; it's about *how* we enter it. How leaders enter spaces sets the process rhythm for everything that follows. It signals whether expertise will be honored, whether questions are welcome, and whether systems are something people comply with or contribute to.

THE EXPERT'S SPACE

When I walk into a classroom, I can show up like I'm the expert in the space, or I can walk in with the awareness that I'm entering *their* expert space. That shift changes everything. It changes the questions I ask, the assumptions I make, and the tone I bring with me. It forces me to pause long enough to understand before I start offering direction. It reminds me that while I may know leadership, they know the landscape. They know the history, the personalities, the timing, the invisible threads that hold the day together.

When I start with curiosity instead of correction, people open up. They talk about why something is happening. They walk me through what they were trying to accomplish. They share the thinking behind the moment, thinking I never would have seen had I led with answers instead of questions. That's when I began to understand how much *trust is built by acknowledging someone else's expertise.* People want to feel seen for what they know. They want the leader in their space to recognize the skill behind what they do. They don't need applause. They don't need a performance review. Most days, they just need to know that the person walking into their room respects the work they've already done.

That realization became even clearer the afternoon I was sweeping the gym with Steve, our custodian. It was my first year leading a building, and I was doing everything I could to learn the school from the inside out. When we finished sweeping, I grabbed the broom and asked where he wanted it. He shrugged and said, "That's probably good there." But something in his voice told me it wasn't good. Not even close. It wasn't where he wanted it. It wasn't how he needed it stored to do his job well. He just didn't want to correct his principal.

So I turned to him and said, "You do this every day. Please...show me exactly what you want." He looked confused at first, but then he smiled a little and I knew we were OK. He didn't just show me *where* the broom went, he explained *why* it went there. The broom was stored next to the door, but higher up on the wall so adults could reach it quickly, but young kids couldn't grab it and turn it into a toy. It was positioned in a spot where it wouldn't be buried under equipment. It sat on the same side of the gym he always accessed because the hallway he cleaned each afternoon connected directly to that corner. The flow mattered. The placement mattered. The details mattered in ways I had never considered. The place where I had put it, on the opposite side of the gym, was not "probably good." It was wrong for the system he had built, wrong for the rhythm he relied on, wrong for the expertise he carried, and when I left, he was going to put it back where it belonged and may have even grumbled under his breath that he had to do one more step in an already full day. *Every system has a rhythm, whether leaders notice it or not.* When we ignore it, we disrupt the work. When we honor it, we strengthen the process.

That small moment changed more than where the broom lived. It changed our conversations. It changed our processes, and it changed our trust. When we later needed to rework the cafeteria flow to get kids out the door faster, Steve was involved in discussing where trash cans should go and how he could adjust his process to accommodate. When we needed to adjust cleaning schedules because some staff were only in the building part-time, he was willing to be the expert in that area and collaborate on the plan. He was the expert in the space, but he shifted from silently knowing how things should run to actively modeling and vocalizing how things could run better. Additionally, I shifted from assuming I understood the environment to actually honoring the environment he had built. I'm sure it also helped him walk away from less conversations thinking, "If they just would have asked me" which is a thought too many people have when we don't include them in the discussions leading up to the decision. When that happens, we set up a pocket of people who start to question the decision, how the decision was made, and how future decisions will be made. The inclusion not only helps in the moment, but when we miss something down the road, those people are willing to come and ask us questions as opposed to keeping the conversations in their pockets. Without it, the building has an undertone of distrust, which can grow behind closed doors without ever knowing it.

What might have looked like a meaningless "tell me where the mop goes" moment was actually setting the foundation for every productive discussion that followed. Because I didn't just acknowledge his expertise, I modeled what it looks like to ask, to listen, and to adjust. From that point forward, our conversations weren't about defending decisions, they were about improving the system together.

Leaders don't lose influence when they acknowledge someone else's expertise. They strengthen it. They build trust. They deepen connection. And they create the conditions for process, the systems, routines, and structures that help people stay aligned, to actually work. Walking into an expert's space with humility isn't a sign of weakness. It's a sign of leadership. And when we do it well, we bridge the gap between people and process, opening the door for the kind of shared ownership that makes everyone better.

> **Walking into an expert's space with humility isn't a sign of weakness. It's a sign of leadership.**

Core Value Connection

Manageable
Tomorrow, in one conversation, ask the person closest to the work to share their thinking before you share yours. Expertise grows when leaders create space rather than fill it.

Meaningful
Identify three spaces where certain voices dominate while others remain quiet. Reflect on which experts need more room to lead and why.

Magnetic
If expertise were shared rather than centered on me, how would our processes improve?

CHAPTER 17

Build Capacity, Not Dependence

Grow leaders, not followers

"The function of leadership is to produce more leaders, not more followers."
— Ralph Nader

I was standing in line at a grocery store recently when the man in front of me placed three items on the conveyor belt. The total popped up on the screen, and then he did something I hadn't seen in years. He reached into his pocket and pulled out a checkbook. Not a card. Not a phone. A full, old-school checkbook. It felt like spotting a rare bird in the wild.

As he started writing the check, something ridiculous happened inside me. I felt myself getting frustrated. Not at him, he did nothing wrong, but at the time it was taking to finish the transaction. Now, we are not talking about a five- or ten-minute process...we are talking about seconds. Twelve to sixteen seconds. The twelve to sixteen seconds I knew it would take him to finish writing. And I actually caught myself thinking, *I'll just pay for his stuff. I'll tell him I've got it, he can head out, and we can all move on with our day.*

In that moment, trying to save those seconds made perfect sense to me. I had nowhere to go. Nothing that was going to thaw out if I didn't get it home faster. I just wanted to get to the next thing in my life and sitting there in line was prohibiting me from doing so. Paying for his things would have got everyone to the next thing, it would have been easier for him to just grab his stuff and move on, easier for the cashier as they could just keep adding things to the bill and only have one transaction, and in that moment nothing really changed for me because I was already going to pay for some stuff. The problem is, I used to lead like that all the time.

This book is organized around the rhythms of leadership, Personal, People, and Process. What I've learned over time is that each of those rhythms contains its own subtle beats. When we start looking at the rhythms and attaching a process to how we act and react, there is more consistency to how we lead. Inside the Process Rhythm, one pattern shows up consistently in the moments when people grow: *Trust → Teach → Transfer.* It's the practical framework that keeps the work human and sustainable. Standing there behind a man writing a check reminded me of the rhythms. As I drove home, having lost sixteen seconds of my life to a paper check, I thought about times in my career when I built trust well and times I didn't. I thought about how teaching isn't always formal instruction, it's the quiet support we offer in the moment when someone needs clarity, not rescue. I thought about the people, like Steve in our building, who taught me that transferring ownership isn't about stepping back, it's about stepping with. Those moments are the reminders that frameworks aren't concepts we post on a wall, they're choices we make in the tiny, ordinary interactions that shape whether people grow or stay stuck.

There were so many times early in my career when someone came to me with something they were unsure about. It was an email to write,

BUILD CAPACITY, NOT DEPENDENCE

a phone call to make, a conversation they needed to have, a form they needed to complete, an agenda that needed to be developed, a situation to sort out…I could honestly type scenarios for pages and when I started leading, they all ended the same. Instead of slowing down to support them, I would just do it myself. Not because they couldn't do it. Not because I didn't trust them. But because I convinced myself it was faster for me to do it and I was being a good leader by taking something off their plate. It was the leadership equivalent of paying for someone's groceries so you don't have to wait sixteen seconds.

Those "I'll do it, don't worry about it" moments weren't saving me time. They were costing me, and essentially everyone in the organization, something much bigger. When I started doing everyone else's work, I inevitably had to stop doing parts of my own. Not intentionally. Not because I didn't care. Just because there are only so many things a person can hold at once.

When I dropped something that was mine to do, people started to question whether I could do the job I had been hired to do. No one saw the invisible work I had quietly done for others. They didn't see the nine things I was working on behind the scenes. They only saw the one thing I missed. That's what dependency does, it hides the effort and exposes the mistake.

It also sends messages we never intend.

"I got it" eventually becomes "You don't need to learn this," which eventually becomes "I don't think you can handle this," which eventually becomes "I don't trust you with this."

That grocery-store moment didn't just remind me of a frustrating checkout line. It reminded me to be aware of the times I still fall back into those old habits. If we want people to lead, grow, and take ownership, then we can't be the hero of every story. What people need is capacity, they don't need to be rescued. That requires a different kind of leadership, leadership grounded in a simple, steady rhythm:

Trust → Teach → Transfer.

> If we want people to lead, grow, and take ownership, then we can't be the hero of every story.

Trust begins when people believe their voice matters, not because we say it does, but because we act in ways that prove it. I had to learn that staff weren't hesitant because they lacked ideas. They were hesitant because they lacked safety. Teaching isn't about giving answers, it's about building confidence. Teaching is slower than doing just like empowering is slower than rescuing. But it's the only way people grow. Transfer is what happens when someone takes the next step *without* waiting for you to validate it. It's when people move from asking for permission to acting with purpose.

The rhythm shows up in random places. For me, it was a regular Tuesday in the building. I was already exhausted before the day even began, and by mid-afternoon I was hoping no one else would walk through my door with anything heavy. Which, of course, meant someone walked through my door with something heavy.

A teacher came in, upset about a parent conversation that had gone sideways. I nodded, listened halfway, and waited for the moment I could jump in with my advice, because providing solutions was leadership, right? Halfway through her explanation, she stopped talking. Not because she was finished, but because she could see I wasn't fully present. She looked at me and said, "I'm not asking you to fix it. I just needed someone to hear me." The sentence hit like a punch. I wasn't listening to understand. I was listening to respond.

Listening to respond vs. listening to understand is the difference between building dependence and building capacity. Responding hands someone an answer. *Understanding hands them confidence.*

BUILD CAPACITY, NOT DEPENDENCE

That conversation caused me to pause. It made me think about all the times someone came to me already carrying the answer but unsure if they were "allowed" to say it out loud. When I immediately responded with a solution I was not only not listening to them, but squashing their input before they even gave it. It made me think about the Build Back Relationships work, how circling back after a hard moment isn't just relational, it's instructional. It clarifies something. It strengthens something. Capacity sits on top of those repairs.

I began to see this more clearly everywhere. A teacher who walked into my office with a question she had already answered in her head three times. A paraprofessional with a brilliant idea who worried it might come across as overstepping. Steve, who knew exactly how to fix the cafeteria flow but had never been asked for his thinking. These people weren't waiting for direction because they lacked motivation. They were waiting because they weren't sure their voice really mattered. Buildings are filled with people who already know what to do, *they just need someone to believe in their ability to say it out loud.*

The Process Rhythm creates consistency for those in the organization, which, as we have talked about, builds trust. Trust creates safety. Teaching creates clarity. Transfer creates ownership. Capacity grows when all three live together.

As I started leaning into this rhythm intentionally, the way I framed conversations changed. I asked different questions. "Tell me more about that?" instead of "Here's what I would do." "Where do you want this to go?" instead of "Let me tell you the next step." "What have you already tried?" instead of "Here's the solution." "What do you need from me so you can solve the problem?" instead of "I'll just do it."

Those questions weren't only strategies, they were signals that said, "I trust you," long before the transfer happened.

Capacity grows in layers. First, people feel safe. Then they feel clear. Then they feel confident enough to step into something bigger. The more I watched this happen, the more I realized that capacity is rarely loud, but it is always visible. You feel it in the way people talk about their work. You see it in the way teams solve issues without waiting for permission. You hear it in the way people reference each other's strengths instead of their own doubts.

And the interesting thing is this: as people grow, the leader's role shifts, too. You're no longer the answer. You're the anchor. You don't need to steer the whole building because everyone is steering their own part of it. The work becomes wider, not heavier.

> Supporting someone through the work will always create more momentum than doing the work for them,

The rhythm shows up everywhere. In conflict, collaboration, classrooms, staff meetings, conversations in hallways during dismissal time for kids. Every time it shows up, it reinforces the same truth: Supporting someone through the work will always create more momentum than doing the work for them, and in the long run, it is the most sustainable way forward.

The shift also starts to reshape the feel of a building. People come into meetings ready, not reluctant. They bring solutions, not just frustrations. They take initiative rather than waiting for permission. They trust themselves because someone trusted them first. That's when the building moves differently, not because one person is leading exceptionally well, but because many people are leading confidently.

Which is why I keep returning to that grocery-store moment. Standing behind a man writing a check and thinking I could save myself sixteen seconds by paying for his groceries is the perfect metaphor for the leadership trap we all fall into. Saving time today can cost capacity tomorrow.

Trust the people in front of you.
Teach in ways that build confidence instead of dependence.
Transfer ownership so leadership spreads, not stalls.

The work you do for people fades the moment you walk away. The work you do with people lasts, and that leaves room for others to lead.

Capacity doesn't just make the work lighter; it makes the work better. When people feel trusted, taught, and empowered, they don't just take ownership of problems; they take ownership of possibilities. They start noticing what's working, naming what's working, and leaning into it with confidence. That's the part of the Process Rhythm that becomes contagious. Because once people believe they can lead, they begin to see greatness in themselves and in each other. When they see it, they start sharing it. That's where momentum really begins. The next chapter builds on that shift, because once capacity grows, one of the most important things a leader can do is help people recognize the good they're creating and extend it far beyond the moment. Leadership doesn't end with building capacity. It continues when we multiply the good that capacity makes possible.

Core Value Connection

Manageable
Tomorrow, when someone brings you a problem, ask, "What do you think your best next step might be?" before offering your perspective. This builds capacity rather than reliance.

Meaningful
Think of two people who rely on you more than they should. Reflect on what patterns in your leadership might be unintentionally contributing to that dependence.

Magnetic
If my goal is to grow leaders who don't need me for every solution, what habit must I change in how I respond?

CHAPTER 18

Multiply the Good

Extend the greatness you see

"What we give power to grows."
—Audre Lorde

There's a point each year, usually after the early energy of a new beginning settles, when routines start to take over. The excitement of the first few weeks gives way to the normal rhythm of the work, and that rhythm often becomes quieter and more isolated than we expect. Even in schools where people collaborate, check in with each other, and share moments throughout the day, most adults still spend the majority of their time in a space with the group they've been assigned. That's where the silos start to form, not intentionally, not maliciously, but simply because the work itself pushes people into individual corners. And while leaders can't eliminate those silos completely, we can put windows in them.

Schools are full of great things happening all the time. Good cultures recognize those things. Great cultures acknowledge the people responsible for them. But the best cultures extend those stories beyond the people who lived them. It makes sure the greatness happening in one room becomes visible in rooms where it wasn't seen.

This is where leadership during the "routine season" becomes something different. Early in the year, leadership is about connection, showing up, being present, building trust. But once the year settles, leadership becomes just as much about connecting people to their people. It's about making sure individuals don't feel like they're operating alone in their own quiet corner of the building. It's about creating windows that let people see what's happening across the school and helping them feel part of something larger than their four walls.

That's why the simple act of noticing matters so much. When you see something good, say something. But don't stop there, say it to one more person. Tell the teacher next door. Mention it to someone down the hall. Bring it to a colleague who wasn't in the room. Maybe most importantly, share it with someone outside the building, the spouse, the partner, the friend, the parent, someone that person goes home to at the end of the day.

When people hear their great work is being talked about beyond the moment, when the story travels to someone who knows them outside the role they play at work, it closes the value gap. It connects what they do to how they feel about what they do. It ties their daily work to the people who reinforce their identity and remind them why the work matters.

The value gap in any organization is real. People feel guilty when they are at work for not being at home. They feel guilty when they are at home for not being at work. This tends to impact the way we walk into both places. As leaders, we may have more access to more places in the building and can be the conduit for connecting stories and closing gaps. When you close that gap, two things happen. The first is that you feel better…you are now the connector of great stories and in a time where you get knocked down for things you may or may not control, you need some wins. The other thing, and more importantly, is that people in the building walk with more purpose into both places.

Purpose isn't created by a motivational speech. It's created when someone feels seen and valued in the spaces they go to daily. It's created when the story of their work doesn't stay trapped inside a classroom or an office but travels to the people who support them at home. It's created when leaders become the bridge between what happens privately and how it is understood collectively.

Leaders sometimes underestimate the power of that bridge. Sharing a good story feels small. Mentioning something positive to a colleague may feel quick and easy. Calling a spouse after school or texting a parent about the incredible work their child's teacher is doing can feel like an extra step. But those small acts become the windows that illuminate the silos. They become the moments people remember on the days routines feel heavy and they add up.

One small acknowledgment becomes a thread. Several threads become a connection. Enough connections become a culture. And culture, at its core, is the feeling people carry when they walk through the doors each day that lead to the behaviors they display. Leaders amplify the purpose already there. They notice it, name it, and make sure it travels. Few leaders articulate this rhythm of noticing and extending more clearly than Dr. Amber Teamann.

Dr. Amber Teamann, Executive Director of Innovation and Technology, co-author of *Lead With Appreciation*, and one of the most thoughtful leaders in my circle, echoes this rhythm with remarkable clarity. Her work keeps coming back to the same truth: people thrive in environments where they feel valued, and intentional appreciation is one of the quickest ways to elevate a school's culture. But what makes her approach different is that appreciation is never generic. It fits inside her framework of being easy, meaningful, and compelling because it starts with truly knowing people.

For Dr. Teamann, appreciation isn't about what the leader gives; it's about how the other person receives. She talks about the difference between a giver mindset and a receiver experience. You can pour praise, recognition, and gratitude into someone all day long, but if it doesn't connect to who they are, some of it will always leak out. She once described it like pouring water into a pot with a hole in the bottom. No matter how much you pour in, some of it drains away. Leadership, then, isn't about pouring faster or louder. It's helping more of it to stay.

When leaders make time to see people where they are, to understand how they want to be seen, valued, and acknowledged, appreciation holds. It lands. It stays. And when appreciation stays, it sharpens a leader's lens, strengthens connection, and turns isolated moments of greatness into shared culture.

Her message affirms the heart of this chapter: greatness is already present. Appreciation is what brings it into the light, extends it beyond the room, and allows it to take root in the culture. And when appreciation becomes part of the way you lead, it naturally carries forward, helping people feel connected not just to you, but also to each other.

I saw this idea come to life years ago when the village of Fall Creek was hit hard by a storm, and the entire town lost power. It was summer, so people weren't thinking about school, but our generators kicked in, giving us power in parts of the building, including the kitchen. Knowing families were in a tough spot, and that refrigerators would start failing, we posted on social media that people could bring any food they worried would spoil. Just put it in a labeled bag and store it at the school until power returned.

Within minutes, we got dozens of messages thanking us. People were relieved, grateful—even emotional. Over the entire stretch of the outage, we received exactly three bags of food. They didn't need to bring their food. They just needed to know they could.

That's the part of multiplying the good that leaders sometimes miss. We assume the impact is in the action. But sometimes the impact is in the assurance. Sometimes people don't need to use the support, you just need to offer it. When people know they have options, their whole relationship with their work, their school, and their community changes. They talk about the school differently. They interpret its intentions differently. They assume the best because they've seen the best, even if they never needed to take advantage of it.

Leadership is full of these moments. And just like recognition, assurance travels. When someone experiences a moment of goodness, even a simple moment of consideration, they tell their people. And when they tell their people, those stories begin to shift how the community sees the work happening inside the building.

Fall in Wisconsin has a way of stopping you. The vibrant leaves, crisp air, and sunlight that hits just right is the kind of beauty that makes you forget for a moment how long winter is going to be. I was passing through a path of bright reds, oranges, and yellows when I caught sight of one tree that had already lost all its leaves. Completely bare. No color, no life, just branches.

And my first thought was, "This is beautiful, but that tree's not looking great."

I stood there in the middle of all that beauty and realized what I had just done. Everything around me was aligned, balanced, extraordinary—and I went straight to the one exception. Straight to the flaw. Straight to the "Yeah, but."

As you can clearly see by now, the things I notice in the world take me right back to how I lead and where I have screwed up. I had been in enough meetings to know the pattern. Someone shares a win:

"We had an incredible lesson today."
And the response, well-meaning and practical is:
"Yeah, it worked, but next week gets harder."
"Yeah, I liked it, but we still need to fix…"
"Yeah, it's a good start, but let's not get ahead of ourselves."

We think we're being realistic. We think we're staying grounded. But what people hear is the erasure of the good. Over time, if we're always the "Yeah, but" leader, people stop bringing us the good altogether. Not because they don't want to share it, but because they want the moment to stay positive, and they've learned that bringing it to us might change its tone.

Multiplying the good means refusing to be the "Yeah, but" leader. It means letting the moment be good. Letting the joy rise without taming it. Letting people feel proud before redirecting them to the next task. When leaders consistently honor the good, people bring them more of it, and they start seeing more of it in each other.

It isn't only about big gestures or community-wide messages. Sometimes it's about noticing your own mindset and how easily a single thought can overshadow what's going well. This happens more than people care to admit in schools. Often, we are our own worst enemies when it comes to what we multiply. The idea that no one is changing the way they talk about us until we change the way we talk about us is real, and when the negative impact is the default in the communication, everyone loses. Think about how many times you hear this in the building when something great happens:

"That's just what I do."
"Well, we were put in a good position, so that's probably why…"
"It's not a big deal."

Every time we do that we diminish the work that we are doing, but we also give the person we are talking to license to do exactly the same. Our words matter…not only to each other, but to those who don't see what we do daily. Being intentional about how we talk about us is a great way to shift the narrative and get momentum moving in the right direction.

This is where recognition becomes part of the process rhythm. When people experience meaningful recognition, not generic praise, but being truly seen, they are more likely to thrive at work. The work multiplies because people multiply it.

That's what happens when you start using the *Recognize → Acknowledge → Extend* framework with your teams. What if every Monday morning during your team meeting, someone on your team told one story. Not one story for each person at the table. Just one story. If there are five people on your administrative team there is a tremendous opportunity right in front of you. The moment a story was shared by one person at the table, the commitment becomes clear: the rest of the group would connect with that person before the next week's meeting. That meant four different leaders seeking out that one staff member, naming their impact, and making sure they knew the story had traveled, and just as importantly, who shared it.

Everyone around that administrative team table will have to make a difficult decision at some point. The response to that difficult decision is often based on every interaction we have had with the person on the other side of that difficult decision leading up to when it takes place. If we, as a team, can help one of our teammates by making sure people in the building know they were being talked about at the administrative team meeting, we give that leader a better chance in difficult decisions down the road.

The shift is immediate. Not because we recognized more people, but because each moment of recognition had four voices behind it. Four leaders extending the same story in four different ways. And over time, something will happen: people will start extending stories on their own. Teachers texting colleagues about small wins. Parents emailing teachers because another teacher told them something positive. The three teachers from Chapter 5 who found me in the hallway to tell me a story about a colleague. When you are consistent in being present and listening and just as consistent in the follow up, it creates momentum for everyone.

Recognize, Acknowledge, Extend became a natural rhythm. It was Manageable. It was Meaningful. It was Magnetic. And right underneath it lived the deeper process rhythm: trust, teach, transfer. The more people were trusted with the story of someone else's greatness, the more they learned how to name greatness themselves. And when that happened, ownership wasn't something I had to promote, it became something they carried.

Seeing the good, naming the good, and extending the good isn't just a feel-good exercise, it's capacity-building. It's identity-building. It's culture-building. Greatness rarely arrives with a spotlight. It walks quietly. It whispers. It slips in through effort and consistency and a thousand invisible moments. Leaders multiply the good by catching those moments early, naming them clearly, and extending them generously. And when we do, people don't just feel appreciated, they feel anchored. They feel connected and capable.

> Seeing the good, naming the good, and extending the good isn't just a feel-good exercise, it's capacity-building.

Multiplying the good doesn't mean ignoring what's wrong. It means giving equal weight to what's right so people have the energy and belief to tackle what needs to get better. It means helping people feel proud of what they're contributing instead of only being aware of what they're missing. It means refusing to allow the exception, the bare tree in a forest of vibrant colors, to define the entire landscape.

When people hear their work being talked about beyond the immediate moment, the next day feels different. Shoulders sit higher. Steps feel steadier. Purpose feels visible rather than assumed. Leaders who understand this don't just connect with people, they connect people to people. They keep the stories alive, keep the windows open, and keep the culture moving even in the quietest, most routine parts of the year.

Core Value Connection

Manageable
Tomorrow, identify one positive practice you observed and share it with one additional person or group who would benefit from seeing it. Extending the good is how culture spreads.

Meaningful
Write down three positive things you've seen recently and reflect on why each one worked and who else needs to see it. Strength grows when it becomes visible.

Magnetic
What part of who we are as a school becomes clearer when I intentionally extend the good—and how could that shape who we become next?

CHAPTER 19

Moments Become Movements

How brief moments turn into cultural shifts

*"Great things are done by a series of
small things brought together."*
—Vincent van Gogh

You never really know which moment people will carry with them for the rest of their lives. We like to think it will be the big speech, the powerful meeting, the perfectly crafted message we rehearsed forty times–but it almost never is. More often, it's something that took thirty seconds. A sentence. A gesture. A look. A smile. A smirk. A pause. Something small enough to miss if you weren't paying attention, but meaningful enough that someone else never forgot it. I learned that from Otto in Chapter 12, when he asked me why I wasn't excited to see him, which I was, but I didn't say it. The most important thing I did for him wasn't tied to a program or a decision. It was that every morning I could, I greeted him by name and told him I was excited to see him. I didn't know it grounded him, or that he walked through the doors smiling and waiting for it to happen. Thirty seconds. That was it. But thirty seconds repeated long enough became part of the way he saw himself.

That's what leaders forget. Small moments accumulate. They repeat. They settle into people. They shift identity. They become the story people tell long after we've forgotten we were even in the story. That's why culture never begins in a staff meeting or on a strategic plan, it begins in the seconds between those things. Culture is built in the hallway pause, the handwritten note, the moment you choose patience instead of urgency, the breath you take before responding, the compliment you give without expecting anything back. Culture isn't a speech, it's a pattern, a rhythm.

When we want those moments to move, we have an opportunity to do so by going beyond the expectation of what people have known to that point. There is definitely a difference between meeting expectations and going beyond them. Meeting expectations builds stability. But going beyond them builds momentum. When we first sent kindergarten placement letters, the expectation was simple: share the teacher's name, the supply list, and the first-day details. Necessary information, nothing more. But the moment we created a kindergarten signing day, just like seniors signing their college scholarship commitments, everything changed. Families talked about it and the story traveled. The same thing happened with diplomas. Signing them was the expectation. Recording myself signing each one and sending that video to the family with a story about what I remembered about the student during their thirteen years in the building was going beyond it. Suddenly that moment wasn't a transaction, it was a memory. Every time we step beyond the expectation, we create a moment people carry with them, and the more of those moments we create, the more movement we generate. One of the clearest examples of this came from a moment I didn't plan or orchestrate.

It happened in 2006, my first year as a principal, when we were hiring a third-grade teacher named Sarah. Two veteran third-grade teachers were helping with interviews, and they believed deeply in her. They came into my office every day asking if we'd heard anything yet.

They worried she would get scooped up by another school if we didn't offer the job immediately. After two full weeks of waiting for district approvals, we finally got the green light. I was standing outside my office when the two teachers walked by and asked for what seemed to be the fourteenth time, "When are you going to offer the job?" And in a moment that was part frustration and part instinct, I said, "Why don't you just make the call?"

They stared at me like I wasn't serious. So I doubled down. I handed them her number, pointed them to my office, and waited outside the door with my secretary. Twenty seconds later, we heard a scream from inside my office. Another scream came a moment later from the phone, it was Sarah celebrating on speaker. When the teachers walked out with tears streaming, they looked up and said, "She said yes." And I remember turning to my secretary and saying, "I'll never not do it like this again." Because what happened wasn't just a job offer, it was a moment. A shared moment that became a story. A story that became a practice. A practice that became a movement. We built our entire hiring culture around that one tiny moment. Kids eventually delivered job offers. Former teachers joined in. Parents helped. Staff members went off-site to welcome people. We didn't create big productions; we connected the offer to something meaningful the candidate had shared. Even people who didn't accept the job offer walked away telling someone else about how we treated people. You can't purchase that kind of reputation. You build it, one moment at a time.

As I watched how that one decision changed the way we hired for the next seventeen years, I started asking myself how moments like that could become systems, not rigid programs, but rhythms that helped us catch more of the little things before they slipped by. They reminded me of conversations I started years ago with a co-author on multiple books, Dr. Tony Sinanis.

Tony Sinanis has always been one of the clearest examples of what it looks like to lead from who you are. Long before he became New

York State Principal of the Year or a superintendent, he was the kind of leader whose impact came from the moments most people overlook. He greets people like they matter, listens like their story is the only one in the room, and shows up in places where most leaders rush through.

When we wrote *Hacking Leadership* together, I saw firsthand how Tony turns tiny touchpoints into trust. His leadership isn't performance-based; it's relationship-based. He builds culture the way people build confidence: through repetition, honesty, and a kind of steady presence that makes others feel seen. Tony never waits for the "big" moment. He creates momentum through consistent, human ones, celebrating a teacher, calling out a student's effort, sending a message at just the right time.

His work reminds me that moments aren't meaningful because they're grand. They're meaningful because they're grounded in who we are. And Tony has spent his entire career proving that who you are, repeated over time, becomes the culture you lead. From literally handing the microphone and camera to students for daily announcements as an elementary principal to being fully invested in creating student groups that have actual roles at the district level, Tony was talking about student voice long before it was part of something people talked about daily. Ownership isn't a concept to him; it is a practice.

What makes Tony's work so powerful was never the platform or the tools. It was the intention behind them. He wanted schools to be better for kids, and knows that the small moments matter. His leadership proves that movements don't start with mandates. They start when someone lives their values out loud, consistently enough that others can't help but want to be part of it.

Watching Tony lead that way pushed me to ask a better question: How do you turn moments like those into rhythms people can feel every single day? That's where activities like *First Five Last Five* took on new meaning for me. With kids, the first five minutes of the day determine whether they feel safe and welcome. The last five determine the story they take home about themselves. If I expected teachers to pay attention to those bookends in classrooms, then I needed to model it in staff meetings. So I asked myself before every meeting, "What am I doing in the first five minutes to help the adults in this room feel loved, supported, and safe?" Sometimes it was a story, sometimes it was a laugh, sometimes it was a moment to breathe together. And before we closed, I asked, "What am I doing in the last five minutes to help them remember why they were here?" Adults were far more willing to disagree with why they were at a meeting than to walk out wondering why they came. Eventually, teachers began creating similar routines in their classrooms, and the emotional steadiness in both spaces shifted.

Once you train yourself to look for these moments, in kids and adults, you begin to notice things you used to walk past. A quiet student raising their hand for the first time all year. A teacher staying late not for recognition, but for clarity. A paraprofessional kneeling by a student's desk until their breathing evens out. A custodian whispering something kind to a kid who thought no one noticed them. A parent sending a brave message. A colleague giving "one more thing" on a day when they didn't have much left. None of these moments make headlines, but they create the culture people want to work in.

Moments become movements when you choose to treat them like they matter. Consistency is the invisible force behind momentum. A teacher gives one encouraging smile, and repeats it. A leader names one moment of greatness, and repeats it. A colleague checks in one time, and repeats it. A kid shows one act of kindness, and repeats it. Repetition is what turns moments into patterns. Patterns become identity and that becomes the culture. It's quiet. It's steady. It's almost invisible. Until suddenly you look around and realize everyone is moving differently, not because you told them to, but because they saw someone else do it first.

Sometimes the moment that becomes a movement isn't emotional at all, it's clarity. I've watched entire groups exhale the minute a decision was finally made. People don't always need the perfect answer; they need direction. Indecision weighs heavier than the decision itself. When a leader finally says, "Here's where we're going," it gives people permission to breathe again. That single moment of clarity often becomes the spark for movement.

Other times, the moment that shifts the room is a result of our vulnerability. When leaders name what's hard instead of pretending everything is fine, it gives everyone else permission to be human, too. When leaders model repairing relationships, staff learn how to repair. When leaders offer grace, people begin to offer grace to each other. Small acts of honesty can move a culture more than a dozen inspirational speeches.

Then there are moments that catch you off guard, like when Jake, our kindergarten "Principal of the Day," bent down to pick up a wrapper in the hallway. It wasn't impressive because he picked up the wrapper. It was impressive because he believed he was doing something we all do. He saw something, acted on it, and believed the identity belonged to him. Adults are no different. When people notice patience, they begin to practice patience. When they notice recognition, they begin offering recognition. They notice ownership and begin taking ownership. All of it builds momentum.

What I've learned after almost thirty years in this work is this: Moments become movements when you treat them like they matter, and movements become culture when you repeat them on purpose. One moment becomes another. One person becomes another. One interaction becomes another. And before you know it, the tiny decisions you made when no one was watching

> **Moments become movements when you treat them like they matter, and movements become culture when you repeat them on purpose.**

become the foundation of who you are as a school, as a team, and as a community. Leadership isn't built on dramatic turning points. It's built on the daily choice to be in the moment in front of you. Moments become movements when they are meaningful and repeated. Leaders who understand that never run out of influence.

Core Value Connection

Manageable
Tomorrow, take one small meaningful moment you've created recently—an encouraging word, a brief recognition, a steady presence, or a shared story—and intentionally repeat it in a similar context with a different person. Not a new initiative. Not a new system. Just repetition with intention.

Meaningful
Write down one moment from this past week that felt aligned with who you want to be as a leader. Then imagine what would happen if that moment became a weekly rhythm rather than a one-time occurrence.

Magnetic
If a single repeated moment could become the next movement in my school, which moment would I choose—and what would repeating it teach people about who we are becoming?

Summary:
The Process Rhythm

The Process Rhythm is where everything you believe and everything you build with people either holds or quietly falls apart. The Personal Rhythm gives you clarity. The People Rhythm gives you trust. But it's the way you design your processes, your habits, routines, systems, and go-to moves, that determines whether your culture can actually sustain itself over time. The processes stick when they fit the identity and people of your organization, and they fall apart when they fight them.

Before leaders ever say a word about mission or vision, the mission is already being modeled. How you walk into a room, how you respond when something goes wrong, what you tolerate, and what you celebrate, those are all processes. They teach people what "good enough" looks like long before any handbook or slogan ever does. Most people don't drift because they're lazy. They drift because there is no clear, lived picture of what "great" looks like in action. That's why modeling can matter more than messaging. When people see excellence, they know how to aim for it. When they only hear about it, they tend to fall back to whatever their default has always been.

This is where manageable, meaningful, and magnetic show up. If a process is manageable, people can actually do it on their hardest days, not just their best. If it's meaningful, it relates to something they care about, not just something on your agenda. If it's magnetic, it connects to other work so it feels like part of a larger story, not just one more extra task. When your systems check those three boxes, effort naturally rises. Hands go higher, not because you demanded more effort, but because people can see themselves in the work.

The Process Rhythm collapses quickly when leaders forget whose space they're in. Every classroom, office, department, or team already has a lived process, a rhythm built by someone who knows that space deeply. When you walk into that space like the only expert in the room, your feedback feels like doubt, not support. When you walk in with the awareness that you're entering their expert space, everything shifts. Your questions change. Your tone changes. The way the moment lands changes. Starting with curiosity instead of correction tells people, "I see your expertise," before you ever offer direction. People want to feel trusted for what they already know. They don't need applause every time you walk in; most days, they just need to know the person in their space respects the work that's already been done.

> Starting with curiosity instead of correction tells people, "I see your expertise," before you ever offer direction.

If Manageable, Meaningful, and Magnetic describe the shape of your processes, then Trust, Teach, and Transfer describe the beat that keeps those processes human. A lot of us fall into the trap of: "I'll just do it. It's faster." It saves you sixteen seconds today but costs you capacity for the next sixteen months or more. When you jump in and handle everything yourself, you don't just exhaust your own bandwidth, you unintentionally send a message that other people can't or shouldn't own the work.

The Process Rhythm pushes you toward a different pattern. Trust begins when people believe their voice matters, not because you've said it does, but because you act in ways that prove it. You ask what

SUMMARY: THE PROCESS RHYTHM

they're already thinking before you hand them your answer. You invite their voice into decisions that affect their work. Teaching comes next, and it isn't always a formal training. Most of the time, it's the way you slow down in real time to support rather than rescue. It's the difference between "I've got it" and "What do you need from me so you can handle this?" Teaching is slower than doing, just like empowering is slower than rescuing, but it's the only way people grow. Transfer is what happens when someone takes the next step without waiting for you to validate it. It's when people move from asking for permission to acting with purpose. When Trust, Teach, and Transfer live together, capacity grows. People stop waiting for you and start leading with you. You're no longer the hero of every process, you're the anchor that makes shared leadership possible.

Processes also give you a chance to multiply what's working, not just manage what's wrong. When leaders build simple rhythms to see, name, and spread the good, they turn isolated wins into shared practices. One small act of recognition becomes a thread. Several threads become a connection. Enough connections become a culture. That's where manageable, meaningful, and magnetic sit right on top of Trust, Teach, and Transfer. A recognition routine, like the one mentioned in administrative team meetings with one story can be manageable because even on our toughest week we can extend one story. It's meaningful when it is specific to someone's identity and effort. It becomes magnetic when it automatically connects to others, when everyone else in the room goes and extends that story to the person who lived it. Underneath that, the trust grows because you're trusting people with the story of someone else's greatness, teaching them how to name what they see, and transferring the work of culture-building from the leader to the entire staff.

In the end, the Process Rhythm is really about what happens to moments. You can treat them like throwaways or treat them like seeds. When you go just to the edge of the expectation, send the basic letter, sign the basic diploma, offer the basic job, you create stability. When you go beyond expectation and turn those ordinary points of contact into intentional experiences, you create momentum. Do it once, and it's a moment. Do it over and over, and it becomes the momentum that people talk about when you are not there..

That's the heart of the Process Rhythm. You take processes that fit your identity. You design them with the people who will actually live them. You make them manageable, meaningful, and magnetic. You move through Trust, Teach, and Transfer so capacity spreads. And when identity, people, and process start to line up, the work doesn't depend on a single charismatic day or a single charismatic leader. It depends on habits that match who you are and who you're becoming, habits people can carry long after you've left the room.

CONCLUSION

We're all in this thing together

> "Small daily improvements are the key
> to staggering long-term results."
> —Robin Sharma

Leadership never follows a clean, linear path. It shifts with the seasons, swings between calm and chaos, and drifts in and out of moments when everything feels aligned…until suddenly it doesn't. In the beginning, I tried to outsmart that reality. I kept searching for the perfect routine. The system that would protect me from surprise and smooth out the messiness of the work. But people aren't predictable, and schools certainly aren't predictable.

- What I learned over time is that leadership has a rhythm, not a formula.
- Routines break the moment the unexpected shows up. Rhythms bend with it.
- Routines depend on everything going as planned. Rhythms steady you when nothing goes as planned.
- Rhythms don't demand perfection; they help you find your footing again when you've lost it.

That's why I stopped trying to build a perfect system and started listening for the patterns that showed up in my best days. The days when I felt grounded, the interactions that moved people forward, the moments when I could feel myself leading from who I was, not who I thought I was supposed to be. When I finally paid attention to that rhythm, everything else became clearer. I understood why some days felt aligned and others felt scattered. I saw where I drifted and where I needed to come back. I started creating consistency not just for myself but also for the people who needed me to be steady even when the world around us wasn't.

> That's why I stopped trying to build a perfect system and started listening for the patterns that showed up in my best days.

Those rhythms—Personal, People, and Process–ended up becoming the backbone of this book.

Not because they are something to memorize, but because they already lived underneath the work. They were the patterns I returned to when I felt lost, the cadence that gave everything shape, the steady beat that helped me show up with purpose even when the day tried to pull me into reaction.

The Personal Rhythm (Intention, Connection, and Direction) is the heartbeat of leadership. It showed up every time I grounded myself before I walked into a tough conversation, every time I reminded myself that people respond to presence before position, every time I chose clarity over chaos. When intention leads, connection deepens. When connection deepens, direction becomes something we walk together instead of pushing alone.

The People Rhythm (Recognize, Acknowledge, and Extend) showed up in hallways, in meetings, in thirty-second moments that changed the way people saw themselves. It's the rhythm that teaches us that people rise because you see them. Recognition builds confidence. Acknowledgment builds identity. Extension builds culture. Every one of those pieces showed up in the stories you've just read.

The Process Rhythm (Manageable, Meaningful, Magnetic) showed up when we turned ideas into practice, when we built systems small enough that real people could actually do them, when we created momentum without adding pressure. It's the rhythm that keeps the work alive after the excitement wears off, the rhythm that helps leaders build something that lasts instead of something that drains.

All three rhythms wove themselves through the stories in this book, sometimes quietly, sometimes obviously, sometimes without me realizing it until much later. What I hope you saw in each chapter is that none of these rhythms depend on title, authority, personality, or perfection. They depend on presence. They depend on awareness and paying attention to the moments other people miss, because in the end, leadership really does come down to moments.

You never really know which moment people will carry with them. You think it's going to be the big speech, the powerful meeting, the carefully crafted message, the presentation you practiced forty times... but it almost never is. More often, it's something that took thirty seconds. A sentence. A gesture. A look. A pause. Something small enough to miss if you weren't paying attention, but meaningful enough that someone else never forgot it.

I've been reminded of that over and over again. I saw it in the student who smiled bigger when I told him I was so excited to see him. I saw it in the two teachers who offered Sarah her job and walked out of my office with tears in their eyes. I saw it in Angela's text message, six words that lifted an entire room. Every time, the moment became something larger. It repeated and took on a life of its own, not because of the moment itself, but because of the meaning someone attached to it.

That's the throughline of every story here: Leadership lives in the moments most people walk past.

As I look back on the work, I realize something I wish I had learned much earlier in my career: you don't get to choose which moment becomes the one someone remembers, but you do get to

> **Leadership lives in the moments most people walk past.**

choose how you show up for it. You do get to choose your rhythm. You do get to choose whether you move through the day on autopilot or with intention.

- The Personal Rhythm makes sure you lead from your core.
- The People Rhythm connects that core to those around you.
- The Process Rhythm provides clarity for everyone.

Put them together and you stop leading from a position; you start leading from who you are.

Acknowledgments

This book exists because of people who were willing to show up fully, before I knew what I was trying to say, and walked with me the whole time.

To Team Sanfelippo… Andrea, Aidan, Kael, and Allie. You have all lived the examples in this book long before it ever had a title. You have carried the quiet weight of the expectations of being the Superintendent's family, the pressures of the job itself, the looks and judgement, the not getting invited to things because of the role I had, while always helping me see who I am when I forget. You've reminded me that presence matters more than perfection, and that who we are when things don't go as planned is what people remember most.

To the educators, leaders, and teams I've worked alongside in Fall Creek and all across the country, thank you for trusting me with your stories. This book is filled with your moments, your choices, and your courage. You've shown me what leadership looks like on ordinary days, in real buildings, with real people.

To the colleagues, editors, and friends who challenged my thinking, sharpened my words, and pushed me to be clearer than I was when this started, this work is better because of you.

And finally, to anyone who picked up this book hoping to lead with more intention and clarity, thank you for caring enough to look inward first. That choice alone already gives you a better chance.

About the Author

Dr. Joe Sanfelippo is a leadership coach, keynote speaker, and retired school superintendent who works with leaders across the country to build clarity, culture, and connection.

After serving communities for twenty-six years as a teacher, counselor, principal and his final twelve years as the Superintendent of the Fall Creek School District in Wisconsin, Joe shifted his focus to supporting leaders in education, healthcare, and business who want to lead with intention and humanity in real, everyday moments. Under his leadership, Fall Creek was twice recognized as an Innovative District by the International Center for Leadership in Education.

Joe is the author of six other books, including the best-selling *Hacking Leadership* and *Lead From Where You Are*, and his work has been recognized by the U.S. Department of Education, *District Administration*, and in 2019, he was named National Superintendent of the Year by *Education Dive*.

At the core of Joe's work is a simple belief: leadership is less about position and more about the choices we make in how we show up for people. He spends his time helping leaders align who they are, how they treat others, and the systems they build, so their leadership is sustainable, human, and real.

Continue the Work

Leadership doesn't live in the big moments we rehearse. It lives in the small ones we often overlook. It's in the way you walk into a room when you're tired. The tone you choose when the answer would be easier to rush. The decision to slow down when everything around you feels fast.

This book was never meant to be an endpoint. If it helped you clarify who you want to be as a leader, the next step is finding ways to practice that clarity with intention and consistency.

For more information on leadership consulting, resources, or all staff connections please visit: **www.jsanfelippo.com**

The rhythms in this book aren't about doing more work, they are about doing the right work more. Leadership isn't something you finish, it's something you practice. The real work happens after the last page, in the moments when you're tired, distracted, or unsure, and still choose how you show up, and when you show up knowing **who** you are, you give yourself a better chance to serve the people you lead.

More from ConnectEDD Publishing

Since 2015, ConnectEDD has worked to transform education by empowering educators to become better-equipped to teach, learn, and lead. What started as a small company designed to provide professional learning events for educators has grown to include a variety of services to help educators and administrators address essential challenges. ConnectEDD offers instructional and leadership coaching, professional development workshops focusing on a variety of educational topics, a roster of nationally recognized educator associates who possess hands-on knowledge and experience, educational conferences custom-designed to meet the specific needs of schools, districts, and state/national organizations, and ongoing, personalized support, both virtually and onsite. In 2020, ConnectEDD expanded to include publishing services designed to provide busy educators with books and resources consisting of practical information on a wide variety of teaching, learning, and leadership topics. Please visit us online at connecteddpublishing.com or contact us at: info@connecteddpublishing.com

Recent Publications:

Live Your Excellence: Action Guide by Jimmy Casas

Culturize: Action Guide by Jimmy Casas

Daily Inspiration for Educators: Positive Thoughts for Every Day of the Year by Jimmy Casas

Eyes on Culture: Multiply Excellence in Your School by Emily Paschall

Pause. Breathe. Flourish. Living Your Best Life as an Educator by William D. Parker

L.E.A.R.N.E.R. Finding the True, Good, and Beautiful in Education by Marita Diffenbaugh

Educator Reflection Tips Volume II: Refining Our Practice by Jami Fowler-White

Handle With Care: Managing Difficult Situations in Schools with Dignity and Respect by Jimmy Casas and Joy Kelly

Disruptive Thinking: Preparing Learners for Their Future by Eric Sheninger

Permission to be Great: Increasing Engagement in Your School by Dan Butler

Daily Inspiration for Educators: Positive Thoughts for Every Day of the Year, Volume II by Jimmy Casas

The 6 Literacy Levers: Creating a Community of Readers by Brad Gustafson

The Educator's ATLAS: Your Roadmap to Engagement by Weston Kieschnick

In This Season: Words for the Heart by Todd Nesloney, LaNesha Tabb, Tanner Olson, and Alice Lee

Leading with a Humble Heart: A 40-Day Devotional for Leaders by Zac Bauermaster

Recalibrate the Culture: Our Why…Our Work…Our Values by Jimmy Casas

MORE FROM CONNECTEDD PUBLISHING

Creating Curious Classrooms: The Beauty of Questions by Emma Chiappetta

Crafting the Culture: 45 Reflections on What Matters Most by Joe Sanfelippo and Jeffrey Zoul

Improving School Mental Health: The Thriving School Community Solution by Charle Peck and Dr. Cameron Caswell

Building Authenticity: A Blueprint for the Leader Inside You by Todd Nesloney and Tyler Cook

Connecting Through Conversation: A Playbook for Talking with Kids by Erika Bare and Tiffany Burns

The Dream Factory: Designing a Purposeful Life by Mark Trumbo

Stories Behind Stances: Creating Empathy Through Hearing "The Other Side" by Chris Singleton

Happy Eyes: Becoming All Things to All People by Ryan Tillman

The Generative Age: Artificial Intelligence and the Future of Education by Alana Winnick

Recalibrate the Culture: Action Guide by Jimmy Casas

Leading with PEOPLE: A Six Pillar Framework for Fruitful Leadership by Zac Bauermaster

A School Leader's Guide to Reclaiming Purpose by Frederick C. Buskey

Foundations of an Elite Culture: Building Success with High Standards and a Positive Environment by David Arencibia

Personalize: Meeting the Needs of All Learners by Eric Sheninger and Nicki Slaugh

The Five Principles of Educator Professionalism: Rebuilding Trust in Schools by Nason Lollar

Words on the Wall: Culturizing Your Classroom For Observable Impact by Jimmy Casas and Cale Birk

School of Engagement: 45 Activities to Ignite Student Learning by Jonathan Alsheimer

Intentional Instructional Moves: Strategic Steps to Accelerate Student Learning by Sherry St. Clair

Overcoming Education: Complex Challenges, Difficult People, and the Art of Making a Difference by Brad R. Gustafson

The Language of Behavior: A Framework to Elevate Student Success by Charle Peck and Joshua Stamper

Whose Permission Are You Waiting For? An Educator's Guide to Doing What You Love by William D. Parker

The Leader You're Not…And Why It's Just As Important As the Leader You Are by Scott Borba

The Growth-Minded Leader by Tyler Cook

Day by Day: 180 Days of Hope and Encouragement by Zac Bauermaster

Make Your Move: For Ambitious People Ready to Live Their Aspirations by Marlon Styles, Jr.

The Hidden Work: What Separates Top Performers From Underachievers by Weston Kieschnick

Lifted to Lead: How a Paraplegic Orphan Rose from the Streets of Saigon to Become an American Leader by Stefan Bean and Kathy Nash

www.ingramcontent.com/pod-product-compliance
Lightning Source LLC
Chambersburg PA
CBHW070623030426
42337CB00020B/3893